THE
SAC AND FOX

THE SAC AND FOX

Nancy Bonvillain

Frank W. Porter III
General Editor

CHELSEA HOUSE PUBLISHERS
New York   Philadelphia

On the cover Sac and Fox women used cradles such as this one, which dates from around 1900, to carry their children.

Chelsea House Publishers
Editorial Director Richard Rennert
Executive Managing Editor Karyn Gullen Browne
Copy Chief Robin James
Picture Editor Adrian G. Allen
Art Director Robert Mitchell
Manufacturing Director Gerald Levine

Indians of North America
Senior Editor Sean Dolan
Native American Specialist Jack Miller

Staff for **THE SAC AND FOX**
Editorial Assistant Annie McDonnell
Designer John Infantino
Picture Researcher Matthew Dudley

3 5 7 9 8 6 4 2

Library of Congress Cataloging-in-Publication Data

Bonvillain, Nancy.
    The Sac and Fox / Nancy Bonvillain.
        p.   cm.—(Indians of North America)
    Includes bibliographical references and index.
    ISBN 0-7910-1684-6
    1. Sauk Indians—History—Juvenile literature.   2. Fox
Indians—History—Juvenile
literature.   I. Title.   II. Series: Indians of North America
(Chelsea House Publishers)
E99.S23B65   1995   94-21846
977.1′004973—dc20   CIP
                                               AC

CONTENTS

INDIANS OF NORTH AMERICA

CHELSEA HOUSE PUBLISHERS

INDIANS OF NORTH AMERICA: CONFLICT AND SURVIVAL

Frank W. Porter III

The Indians survived our open intention of wiping them out, and since the tide turned they have even weathered our good intentions toward them, which can be much more deadly.

John Steinbeck
America and Americans

When Europeans first reached the North American continent, they found hundreds of tribes occupying a vast and rich country. The newcomers quickly recognized the wealth of natural resources. They were not, however, so quick or willing to recognize the spiritual, cultural, and intellectual riches of the people they called Indians.

The Indians of North America examines the problems that develop when people with different cultures come together. For American Indians, the consequences of their interaction with non-Indian people have been both productive and tragic. The Europeans believed they had "discovered" a "New World," but their religious bigotry, cultural bias, and materialistic world view kept them from appreciating and understanding the people who lived in it. All too often they attempted to change the way of life of the indigenous people. The Spanish conquistadores wanted the Indians as a source of labor. The Christian missionaries, many of whom were English, viewed them as potential converts. French traders and trappers used the Indians as a means to obtain pelts. As Francis Parkman, the 19th-century historian, stated, "Spanish civilization crushed the Indian; English civilization scorned and neglected him; French civilization embraced and cherished him."

7

Nearly 500 years later, many people think of American Indians as curious vestiges of a distant past, waging a futile war to survive in a Space Age society. Even today, our understanding of the history and culture of American Indians is too often derived from unsympathetic, culturally biased, and inaccurate reports. The American Indian, described and portrayed in thousands of movies, television programs, books, articles, and government studies, has either been raised to the status of the "noble savage" or disparaged as the "wild Indian" who resisted the westward expansion of the American frontier.

Where in this popular view are the real Indians, the human beings and communities whose ancestors can be traced back to ice-age hunters? Where are the creative and indomitable people whose sophisticated technologies used the natural resources to ensure their survival, whose military skill might even have prevented European settlement of North America if not for devastating epidemics and disruption of the ecology? Where are the men and women who are today diligently struggling to assert their legal rights and express once again the value of their heritage?

The various Indian tribes of North America, like people everywhere, have a history that includes population expansion, adaptation to a range of regional environments, trade across wide networks, internal strife, and warfare. This was the reality. Europeans justified their conquests, however, by creating a mythical image of the New World and its native people. In this myth, the New World was a virgin land, waiting for the Europeans. The arrival of Christopher Columbus ended a timeless primitiveness for the original inhabitants.

Also part of this myth was the debate over the origins of the American Indians. Fantastic and diverse answers were proposed by the early explorers, missionairies, and settlers. Some thought that the Indians were descended from the Ten Lost Tribes of Israel, others that they were descended from inhabitants of the lost continent of Atlantis. One writer suggested that the Indians had reached North America in another Noah's ark.

A later myth, perpetrated by many historians, focused on the relentless persecution during the past five centuries until only a scattering of these "primitive" people remained to be herded onto reservations. This view fails to chronicle the overt and covert ways in which the Indians successfully coped with the intruders.

All of these myths presented one-sided interpretations that ignored the complexity of European and American events and policies. All left serious questions unanswered. What were the origins of the American Indians? Where did they come from? How and when did they get to the New World? What was their life—their culture—really like?

In the late 1800s, anthropologists and archaeologists in the Smithsonian Institution's newly created Bureau of American Ethnology in Washington,

D.C., began to study scientifically the history and culture of the Indians of North America. They were motivated by an honest belief that the Indians were on the verge of extinction and that along with them would vanish their languages, religious beliefs, technology, myths, and legends. These men and women went out to visit, study, and record data from as many Indian communities as possible before this information was forever lost.

By this time there was a new myth in the national consciousness. American Indians existed as figures in the American past. They had performed a historical mission. They had challenged white settlers who trekked across the continent. Once conquered, however, they were supposed to accept graciously the way of life of their conquerors.

The reality again was different. American Indians resisted both actively and passively. They refused to lose their unique identity, to be assimilated into white society. Many whites viewed the Indians not only as members of a conquered nation but also as "inferior" and "unequal." The rights of the Indians could be expanded, contracted, or modified as the conquerors saw fit. In every generation, white society asked itself what to do with the American Indians. Their answers have resulted in the twists and turns of federal Indian policy.

There were two general approaches. One way was to raise the Indians to a "higher level" by "civilizing" them. Zealous missionaries considered it their Christian duty to elevate the Indian through conversion and scanty education. The other approach was to ignore the Indians until they disappeared under pressure from the ever-expanding white society. The myth of the "vanishing Indian" gave stronger support to the latter option, helping to justify the taking of the Indians' land.

Prior to the end of the 18th century, there was no national policy on Indians simply because the American nation had not yet come into existence. American Indians similarly did not possess a political or social unity with which to confront the various Europeans. They were not homogeneous. Rather, they were loosely formed bands and tribes, speaking nearly 300 languages and thousands of dialects. The collective identity felt by Indians today is a result of their common experiences of defeat and/or mistreatment at the hands of whites.

During the colonial period, the British crown did not have a coordinated policy toward the Indians of North America. Specific tribes (most notably the Iroquois and the Cherokee) became military and political pawns used by both the crown and the individual colonies. The success of the American Revolution brought no immediate change. When the United States acquired new territory from France and Mexico in the early 19th century, the federal government wanted to open this land to settlement by homesteaders. But the Indian tribes that lived on this land had signed treaties with European governments assuring their title to the land. Now the United States assumed legal responsibility for honoring these treaties.

At first, President Thomas Jefferson believed that the Louisiana Purchase contained sufficient land for both the Indians and the white population. Within a generation, though, it became clear that the Indians would not be allowed to remain. In the 1830s the federal government began to coerce the eastern tribes to sign treaties agreeing to relinquish their ancestral land and move west of the Mississippi River. Whenever these negotiations failed, President Andrew Jackson used the military to remove the Indians. The southeastern tribes, promised food and transportation during their removal to the West, were instead forced to walk the "Trail of Tears." More than 4,000 men, woman, and children died during this forced march. The "removal policy" was successful in opening the land to homesteaders, but it created enormous hardships for the Indians.

By 1871 most of the tribes in the United States had signed treaties ceding most or all of their ancestral land in exchange for reservations and welfare. The treaty terms were intended to bind both parties for all time. But in the General Allotment Act of 1887, the federal government changed its policy again. Now the goal was to make tribal members into individual landowners and farmers, encouraging their absorption into white society. This policy was advantageous to whites who were eager to acquire Indian land, but it proved disastrous for the Indians. One hundred thirty-eight million acres of reservation land were subdivided into tracts of 160, 80, or as little as 40 acres, and allotted tribe members on an individual basis. Land owned in this way was said to have "trust status" and could not be sold. But the surplus land—all Indian land not allotted to individuals—was opened (for sale) to white settlers. Ultimately, more than 90 million acres of land were taken from the Indians by legal and illegal means.

The resulting loss of land was a catastrophe for the Indians. It was necessary to make it illegal for Indians to sell their land to non-Indians. The Indian Reorganization Act of 1934 officially ended the allotment period. Tribes that voted to accept the provisions of this act were reorganized, and an effort was made to purchase land within preexisting reservations to restore an adequate land base.

Ten years later, in 1944, federal Indian policy again shifted. Now the federal government wanted to get out of the "Indian business." In 1953 an act of Congress named specific tribes whose trust status was to be ended "at the earliest possible time." This new law enabled the United States to end unilaterally, whether the Indians wished it or not, the special status that protected the land in Indian tribal reservations. In the 1950s federal Indian policy was to transfer federal responsibility and jurisdiction to state governments, encourage the physical relocation of Indian peoples from reservations to urban areas, and hasten the termination, or extinction, of tribes.

Between 1954 and 1962 Congress passed specific laws authorizing the termination of more than 100 tribal groups. The stated purpose of the termination policy was to ensure the full and complete integration of Indians into American society. However, there is a less benign way to interpret this legislation. Even as termination was being discussed in Congress, 133 separate bills were introduced to permit the transfer of trust land ownership from Indians to non-Indians.

With the Johnson administration in the 1960s the federal government began to reject termination. In the 1970s yet another Indian policy emerged. Known as "self-determination," it favored keeping the protective role of the federal government while increasing tribal participation in, and control of, important areas of local government. In 1983 President Reagan, in a policy statement on Indian affairs, restated the unique "government is government" relationship of the United States with the Indians. However, federal programs since then have moved toward transferring Indian affairs to individual states, which have long desired to gain control of Indian land and resources.

As long as American Indians retain power, land, and resources that are coveted by the states and the federal government, there will continue to be a "clash of cultures," and the issues will be contested in the courts, Congress, the White House, and even in the international human rights community. To give all Americans a greater comprehension of the issues and conflicts involving American Indians today is a major goal of this series. These issues are not easily understood, nor can these conflicts be readily resolved. The study of North American Indian history and culture is a necessary and important step toward that comprehension. All Americans must learn the history of the relations between the Indians and the federal government, recognize the unique legal status of the Indians, and understand the heritage and cultures of the Indians of North America.

Many of the earliest and best portrayals of the Sac and Fox were painted by George Catlin. This is Catlin's portrait of Black Hawk, perhaps the most famous leader of the Sac.

ROOTS
OF
AN
ALLIANCE

By the middle of the 18th century, the Sac and the Fox were living in what are now the states of Ohio, Illinois, and Michigan. They were two distinct tribes, but their common experiences brought them together. At first they were friendly neighbors; later they became close allies. Finally, they joined together as a united people.

The Sac and Fox built large towns with spacious streets between rows of lodges made of wood and bark. Outside the village lay their fertile farmland. A famous Sac leader named Black Hawk, who was born in 1767, described his homeland in Ohio in these words:

> In front [of the village], a prairie
> extended to the bank of the
> Mississippi River; and in our rear, a
> continued bluff, gently ascending
> from the prairie. On the side of the
> bluff we had our corn-fields,
> extending about two miles up,

running parallel with the Mississippi. The land around our village, uncultivated, was covered with blue-grass, which made excellent pasture for our horses. Several fine springs broke out on the bluff, near by, from which we were supplied with good water. The rapids of the Rock River furnished us with an abundance of excellent fish, and the land, being good, never failed to produce good crops of corn, beans, pumpkins, and squashes.

Although the Sac and Fox had strong ties to the lands they occupied in the 18th century, they had lived in other locations before that time. Both the Sac and the Fox originally resided in eastern Michigan. The Sac lived in the upper peninsula of Michigan. In their own language, they called themselves *asakiwaki* (a-SAK-ee-wa-kee) or "people of the outlet." This name refers to their location at the

A 19th-century landscape of the Sac and Fox homeland near the Bad Axe River. Like many other Native American peoples, the Sac and Fox were uprooted many times for many different reasons: as a result of warfare between other Native American peoples, because of population pressures caused by the arrival of white settlers and the migrations of other Native Americans, and because of white desire for their land.

outlet of the Saginaw River. The Fox settled in a region south of the Sac, in southern Michigan and northwestern Ohio. Their name for themselves was *mesh-kwakihaki* (mesh-KWA-kee-ha-kee) or "red earths." This label possibly refers to the rich earth of their homeland.

The Sac and Fox were always on friendly terms. They often visited and traded goods with each other. The two tribes remained in their original territory for many years. But the arrival of other Native Americans and of European peoples led the Sac and Fox to relocate.

The Sac and Fox thus shared an experience that was common throughout North America after the Europeans came to the continent. When Europeans arrived in North America they settled on land that originally belonged to Indian tribes. Conflicts often erupted when native peoples resisted the loss of their territory. Since the Europeans had more powerful weapons than did the Indians, they were usually the victors. The Indians who survived the conflicts with Europeans were forced to move westward, away from European settlements in the East. But when the Indians migrated west, they came upon land held by other native groups. In the eastern part of the country, the relocation of Native American peoples began shortly after their first contact with Europeans in the 17th century and continued into the latter years of the 19th century.

When Indian peoples moved west, new hostilities sometimes developed among the native groups. During the middle of the 17th century, both the Sac and Fox came into contact with a powerful confederacy of eastern Indians called the Iroquois. The Iroquois lived in what is now New York State. In the early 17th century, they became involved in the lucrative European fur trade in the Northeast. The Iroquois traded beaver furs to Dutch, British, and French merchants who had recently arrived in North America. Many other native peoples also traded with the Europeans. The Dutch, British, and French were rivals, and each tried to persuade Indian tribes to trade only with them. The Iroquois became allies of the British, although they traded with French merchants as

Native Americans hunt fish by torchlight. The Sac and Fox traditionally made their homes in well-watered lands that were rich in game and fish and fertile for farming.

Whites were not the only enemies of Native American peoples; Indian nations frequently fought against one another as well. This early 19th-century illustration depicts a battle between the Sac and Fox and the Ojibwa. The Sac and Fox had both friends and enemies among their many different Native American neighbors.

well. As a result of competition among European traders, rivalries among their Indian allies also arose. Conflicts and warfare often erupted. In a short time, the Iroquois became a dominant force in the region because of their success in warfare against other Indian peoples. They were able to control much of the fur trade along the Hudson and St. Lawrence rivers in the Northeast.

Despite the Iroquois's military success, they faced problems. By the latter years of the 17th century, the number of beaver in Iroquois territory had decreased considerably. The Iroquois then sent their hunters and warriors to lands farther west in search of new supplies of furs to trade to the Europeans. As the Iroquois ranged west, they came to the territories of many different

Indian tribes. They often launched raids against these groups in order to gain access to their hunting territories. Some Indian peoples fought against the Iroquois while others left their own lands and resettled elsewhere.

By the time the Iroquois came to the region of eastern Michigan in the middle of the 17th century, both the Sac and the Fox had heard of them. The Sac and Fox knew that the Iroquois usually defeated the tribes they met so they decided that it was best to leave the area and escape possible disaster. They headed northwest and soon settled in present-day Wisconsin west of Lake Michigan and south of Lake Superior. The Sac built their villages near Green Bay. And the Fox settled along the Wolf River in northeastern Wisconsin. They ranged as far as Lake Superior in the north, to Lake Michigan in the east, and to the Mississippi River in the south.

In their new locations, the Sac and Fox established friendly relations with most of their Indian neighbors. An Indian group called the Kickapoo lived to the east of the Sac and Fox. The Potawatomi were a numerous tribe living to the west. To the north lived the Winnebago and the Menomini and to the south, the Miami and Illinois.

All of these tribes were distinct groups. Each had its own history and local traditions. However, they also shared many important features of culture. They all spoke languages that belong to the Algonquian family. The languages spoken by the Sac, Fox, and their neighbors were closely related. Although they were separate languages, some words were common to all. They also had many similar rules of grammar. Linguists today believe that the similarities between the languages of the Sac and the Fox indicate that the two had a common historical origin in the distant past, perhaps thousands of years ago.

The Sac and Fox shared additional cultural practices and beliefs. They both lived in large villages and built their lodges on the same design of wooden poles and logs covered with elm bark. They had the same type of economy based on a combination of farming, hunting, and gathering wild fruits and plants. Many of their religious beliefs were also alike.

Because of the numerous similarities in their ways of living, the Sac and Fox were able to maintain good relations with each other. In the 18th and 19th centuries, historical events drew them even closer together. They became allies and often depended on each other for aid and protection from their enemies.

The Sac and Fox became enemies of some of the Indian tribes who lived in the region of the upper Midwest. Their enemies included the Chippewa, Ottawa, and Lakota. These peoples resented the intrusion of the Sac and the Fox into territory near their own. The two groups of enemies often raided each other as each tried to defend its own hunting lands. Conflicts and raids led to even greater animosity.

Difficulties also arose for the Sac and the Fox with some of the European traders who ventured into the upper Midwest in the 17th and 18th centuries. The Fox and the French became bitter enemies and often fought against one another.

In such a climate, the Sac and Fox came to rely on each other for support. Their alliance grew stronger in the 19th century, and although they identified themselves as separate groups until the latter years of that century, their experiences brought them even closer together. The Sac and Fox eventually formed a common cultural and legal entity. They now live as a united tribe on three reservations in Oklahoma, Kansas and Nebraska, and Iowa. The histories of the Sac and Fox have thus brought the tribes together and have merged their present and their future. ▲

One of the earliest known European depictions of a Native American village. With their orderly rows of lodges, nearby fields, and open ceremonial and public areas, traditional Sac and Fox villages would not have been much different from the settlement depicted here.

SAC
AND
FOX
TRADITIONS

The Sac and Fox practiced the traditions that their ancestors had valued for many centuries. They labored at their work, engaged in discussion and collective decision making about village matters, performed religious ceremonies, and visited relatives and friends.

In the 18th century, the Sac and Fox made their homes along the rivers of northern Ohio and southern Michigan. The Sac built a large village named Saukenuk on a point of land between the Mississippi and Rock rivers. Saukenuk was their principal settlement, although some Sac lived in several smaller communities nearby. The village of Saukenuk contained more than 100 lodges, with a population of between 2,000 and 3,000. In 1766, Saukenuk was described by an English traveler named Jonathan Carver as "the largest and best built Indian town," with "regular and spacious streets." Residents of Saukenuk made up approximately half of the total population of the Sac, who at that time numbered some 4,000 or 5,000.

The Fox resided in several villages in an area beginning at the mouth of the Rock River in Ohio and then spreading north along the Mississippi River as far as the present-day city of Prairie du Chien in Wisconsin. The two largest Fox villages of the period contained some 20 to 35 lodges, arranged in parallel rows. The open areas in the Fox towns were used for public events, such as dances and athletic contests. The Fox at that time were less numerous than the Sac, numbering 2,000 or 3,000.

The settlements of both the Sac and the Fox were all located near rivers and streams. The people chose those sites because the land near these waterways was fertile and well-suited for farming. In addition, the streams and rivers were filled with many species of fish, which were an important part of the people's diet.

This is one of Catlin's most famous works; it depicts several Sac and Fox warriors. An easterner by birth and a lawyer by training, Catlin spent much of the 1830s and 1840s traveling the American West in order to paint its native inhabitants. He was especially well acquainted with the Sac and Fox.

The economy of the Sac and Fox was based on farming, hunting, fishing, and gathering wild fruits and plants. Men and women divided the work, and each had assigned tasks to perform. Sac and Fox women were the farmers. Their major crops included varieties of corn, beans, squashes, pumpkins, and melons. These were the staples of the Sac and Fox diet. Sac women planted more than 800 acres of prairie with their crops. The Fox farmed a somewhat smaller area of land. But since they both produced more than enough food for their own households, they traded their surplus to other peoples.

In order to supplement the diet of farm products, women gathered wild fruits and plants growing in nearby fields and forests. They especially prized numerous varieties of wild berries, apples, plums, and nuts. They gathered honey from beehives and several kinds of tubers growing naturally in the earth. In addition, Sac and Fox women caught fish from the waterways in their territory.

Men's work included fishing and hunting. They caught many species of fish that were abundant in the Mississippi and Rock rivers and in smaller streams and lakes. Men often worked together so that they could help each other spread the fishing nets and haul in the catch.

Sac and Fox men hunted animals in the woods and prairies near their villages. Men hunted large animals such as deer, buffalo, and elk, and they caught smaller game including muskrat, raccoon, beaver, and rabbit.

In addition to fishing and hunting, Sac and Fox men traded with neighboring peoples. They mainly exchanged their corn and animal skins for other goods.

The Sac and Fox valued animals for their meat and for other products that were used for many purposes. They made containers from animal skins to store foods and personal possessions. And they used animal bones for handles and blades. In addition, the people's clothing was made from the hides of such animals as deer. Women were responsible for making the clothing. First, they softened the deerskins so that they could be cut and shaped. Then the women made leggings and dresses for themselves and leggings, shirts, and breechcloths for the men. Both women and men covered themselves with warm deerskin robes in the cold winter months.

Sac and Fox men and women often wore jewelry and decorations. They

Catlin's portrayal of Native Americans hunting deer from birch-bark canoes. The Sac and Fox homeland was almost unimaginably rich in game, and its many waterways provided convenient transportation routes.

liked necklaces, armbands, and earrings. Sac men decorated their faces with painted designs using red, blue, and yellow pigments. Among the Fox, both women and men painted and tattooed their faces.

The houses built by the Sac and Fox were rectangular in shape. Several related families lived in each house. Each family had separate living quarters within the lodge. The houses were large, extending some 40 to 60 feet in length and 20 feet in width. They were made of wooden poles and frames, covered with branches and bark from elm trees. The people built wooden benches along the interior walls for sitting and sleeping. They also stored their possessions on or under the benches. Cooking fires were placed in a row down the center of the lodge.

All of the families who lived together in a house were related to each other. Among the Sac, the people typically lived with male relatives. Fathers and their sons or groups of brothers formed the basis of most households. When a man married, his wife came to live with him in his house. A household thus often consisted of elder parents, their unmarried daughters, their sons, and their sons' families.

Among the Fox, people most often resided with the wife's family. After marriage, a Fox woman remained with her own kin while her husband moved in and joined the household. A Fox couple always stayed with the wife's family until the birth of their first child. Afterward, they could live with the husband's

family if they so chose. A couple might make that choice if the wife had many sisters, making the household large. If she had a small family, the couple usually remained with her kin. According to Fox custom, the lodges, furnishings, and other goods within the lodge belonged to the women of the household.

In Sac and Fox marriages, husband and wife cooperated with each other in carrying out their work and their responsibilities. Most marriages were stable, but if the couple were unhappy, they were free to separate and seek new mates.

Sac and Fox men and women usually married when they were about 20 years old. According to custom followed by both the Sac and Fox, when a young man wished to marry, he first conveyed his intention to his mother. She then spoke to the mother of the woman her son hoped to marry. On an appointed night, the young man entered the woman's lodge holding a piece of burning bark and went to the place where the woman was sleeping. When she awakened, she had the choice of accepting or rejecting the man's proposal. If she accepted, she blew out the fire. Among the Sac, the young man then left the lodge and returned in the morning. The Fox man was permitted to remain through the night. In both cases, he was thereafter accepted as a new son-in-law.

If the woman did not wish to marry her suitor, she did not blow out the fire. The man might try a second time. He returned the next day, sat outside the

Karl Bodmer was another accomplished artist who was fascinated by the native peoples of North America. In 1833–34, he painted these two Sac and Fox warriors. Sac and Fox men often decorated their faces as a sign of their valor and prowess as hunters and in raids against other tribes.

woman's lodge, and played love songs on a flute. After playing courting songs all day, he returned at night and hoped that the woman had changed her mind. If she agreed, the couple was married. If not, the man realized that his proposal was unwelcome.

Sac and Fox marriages were relatively simple in ceremony. The families of the couple celebrated the union by exchanging valuable gifts. Afterward the entire community recognized the couple as married.

The Sac and Fox both had systems of kinship based on social units called clans. A clan is a grouping of people who consider themselves related through descent from a common ances-

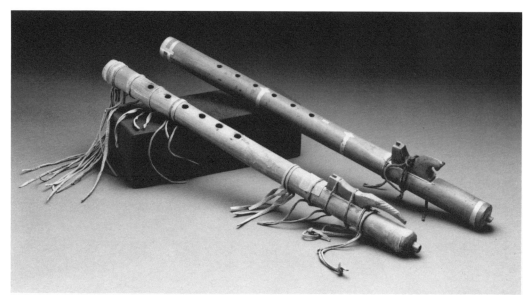

The Sac and Fox made music for ceremonial purposes with flutes, rattles, and drums, which they fashioned from wood and animal skins. Shown here are two 19th-century Sac and Fox flutes.

tor. Since clans include a large number of people, individuals cannot trace their exact relationship to all others in the clan, but they believe that they are related. The Sac had 12 such clans. Each clan was named after an animal, bird, or fish, such as Bear, Wolf, Bald Eagle, Bass, and Sturgeon. The Fox had eight clans, also named after animals, birds, or fish. They included the clans of Bear, Fox, Wolf, Swan, Partridge, Elk, and Black Bass. One Fox clan was named after the natural force of Thunder. Among both the Sac and Fox, when a child was born, she or he became a member of her or his father's clan. This system of descent is called patrilineal, from *patri-*, meaning "father," and *-lineal*, meaning "line" or "descent."

Sac and Fox clans had an important role in determining an individual's choice of spouse. It was impossible to marry someone of one's own clan. Therefore, wives and husbands always belonged to different clans.

Each Sac and Fox clan owned a stock of personal names. Children were given their names shortly after birth from among those belonging to their clan. Since names from each clan differed from all others, people knew the clan identity of any individual from his or her personal name.

Clans also had some ritual functions in Sac and Fox society. Each clan performed an important ceremony twice a year to honor sacred possessions, which were stored in a special bag or bundle.

These possessions consisted of objects having religious meaning to the group. They were tokens of good fortune, such as animal claws, animal teeth, or eagle feathers. Members of a clan considered the objects in its sacred bundle to be powerful healing medicines.

In addition to clans, the Sac and Fox each had another social grouping, which divided all of the people into two sections. One section was represented by the color black and the other by white. Children became members of a division by the order of their birth. Among the Sac, a firstborn child was a member of the black group, the second of the white, the third of the black, and so on. The Fox had a slightly different method of assigning members to the black and white groups. Children alternated by birth, but the first child was assigned to the division opposite the one to which his or her father belonged. Therefore, if the father was black, the first child was white, the next black, and so on. If the father was white, the first child was black, and the subsequent children alternated in color according to the established pattern.

All Sac and Fox children were treated with love and affection by their parents and other relatives. When a woman became pregnant, she was made to follow a number of rules or taboos in order to assure an easy birth and a healthy child. A pregnant woman was forbidden to touch a dead person. If she looked at a corpse, she had to do so with a straight look. The Sac and Fox believed that if a pregnant woman were to glance at a corpse with a slanted gaze, her baby would be born cross-eyed. According to another taboo, if a pregnant woman had to carry firewood, she should do so by carrying the load on her back rather than in her arms. If she followed the rule, she would have an easy birth. If not, her labor would be much more difficult. During pregnancy, a couple was not supposed to engage in sexual relations. If they did so, their baby would be sickly.

When a pregnant woman realized that her child was about to be born, she left her usual lodge and went to a special hut that her relatives had built for her. Several of her female relatives stayed with her in the birth lodge and awaited the birth.

If the birth proved to be difficult for the mother, the family called for the assistance of a special woman who was skilled in healing. The healer gave the expectant mother medicines and performed a number of rituals that the people believed would make the birth easier.

Such a birth was described in an autobiography of a Fox woman, recorded in 1918 when she was quite elderly. She recalled the difficult birth of her first child:

> When that woman [the healer] came, she at once boiled some medicine. After she had boiled it, she said: "Let her sit up for a while. You must hold her so that she will not fall over." After I was made to sit up, she spat upon my head; and she gave me the medicine to drink. After she had given me the medicine, she began singing.

She started to go out singing and went around the little lodge singing. When she danced by where I was, she knocked on the side. "Come out if you are a boy," she would say. And she would again begin singing. When she danced by she again knocked the side. "Come out if you are a girl," she would say again. After she sang four times in a circle, she entered the lodge. And she gave me medicine to drink. "Now it will be born. She may lie down." Lo, sure enough, my baby was born.

New mothers and their babies remained in the birth lodges for at least 10 days. In some cases, they stayed there longer, perhaps as long as one month. After the mother and child returned to their usual lodge, the parents gave a feast to celebrate the birth. Many relatives and village residents attended in order to honor the new baby and his or her family. At that time, a name was given to the child. According to custom, the name was chosen from among the stock of names belonging to the clan of the baby's father.

Young children spent most of their time in play with other children. But as they grew, they gradually began to learn the skills that would be necessary later in life. By the age of six or seven, they were taught to help their parents in certain tasks. Girls learned to plant and weed the gardens, cook food, and sew moccasins. Boys were taught to make bows and arrows and to help their fathers hunt and fish.

The Sac and Fox also taught their children about the responsibilities of adulthood. Puberty was recognized as an important stage in life. A girl's passage to womanhood was marked in special ways. In the autobiography of the Fox woman, she vividly described her mother's teachings:

And then I was thirteen years old. "Now is the time when you must watch yourself; at last you are nearly a young woman. At the time when you are a young woman, you are to hide yourself. Do not come into your lodge. That is what you are to do."

When it happened, I went and laid down in the middle of the thick forest there. I was crying, as I was frightened. After a while my mother got tired of waiting for me. She came to seek me. Soon she found me.

"Come, stop crying. Nothing will happen to you. I shall go and make a lodge for you."

Then, according to custom, the young woman stayed in her special lodge for ten days. During that time, her mother, grandmother, and other female relatives visited her. They brought her food and new clothing. Her grandmother stayed with her and taught her many lessons:

"My grandchild," she would say to me, "soon I shall tell you how to live an upright life. Today you see how old I am. I did exactly what I was told. I tried and thought how to live an upright life. That is the way you should do, if you listen to me as I instruct you."

A Sac and Fox woman with her child in a papoose. Though the photograph is relatively modern, the papoose is of a fairly traditional design and functioned both as a kind of crib or cradle and as a means of transport. The infant could sleep in it while his mother was working; for transport, the papoose would be strapped to the mother's back with the infant in an upright position.

The girl's grandmother told her about many taboos that she must follow during her periods of menstruation. The grandmother told the girl not to touch her hair lest it fall off and not to eat sweet or sour foods lest her teeth fall out. She also told the girl not to talk too much to the boys who might begin to court her. Finally, the grandmother instructed the girl to be kind to others, to be generous and helpful, and to speak politely to all.

After 10 days had passed, the young woman was told to go to the river and bathe. She then dressed in new garments and returned to her family's lodge.

All Sac and Fox girls followed the same procedures at their age of puberty. These behaviors prepared the girls for the responsibilities of adulthood. Boys, too, were taught lessons when they reached maturity. They were encouraged to conduct themselves well and to be kind, generous, and helpful to others. In all cases, young women and men were welcomed into their communities as responsible and valued adults.

The Sac and Fox showed their respect for others at the time of death as well as in life. When someone died, the sad event was announced publicly in the village by a special messenger. Then members of the deceased's clan gathered and mourned the death throughout the night. The body of the deceased was prepared for burial by men belonging to any clan except that of the deceased. The Sac and Fox realized that members of the deceased's own clan were in deep grief and therefore should not be burdened by other responsibilities.

The Sac and Fox buried their dead in graves dug in the ground. The graves of clan members were located near one another. The dead were placed in the grave with the feet pointed toward the West. This is the direction in which souls of the dead were believed to travel on their journey to the afterworld.

Relatives of the deceased placed various objects in the grave to accompany the dead in the afterlife. They left items of clothing and utensils, and they put some food and water in the grave to nourish the soul on its journey.

The grave was then covered with a small wooden shed. A post was erected at the head of the grave and painted with a symbol representing the deceased's clan. At the end of the funeral, a speaker talked to the deceased's soul, asking it to travel away on its journey. The speaker told the soul not to envy the living.

Funerals were followed by long periods of mourning. The Sac and Fox observed mourning restrictions for six months to one year, depending on the closeness in relationship between the mourner and the deceased. Spouses of the deceased and parents of children who died young kept the longest mourning periods. During this time, mourners did not attend to their appearance or attire. Their hair was unkempt and they dressed in shabby clothing. They did not talk much, laugh, or socialize with others. Mourners did not engage in their usual economic activities. Women did no farming and men did no hunting.

Like many other Native American peoples, the Sac and Fox had various rituals associated with the onset of puberty in young men and women. During their first menstruation, young women were isolated in lodges set aside for that purpose.

At the end of the mourning period, the clan of the deceased adopted someone as a symbolic replacement for the relative they had lost. They usually chose a friend of the deceased to have this honor. Members of the deceased's clan celebrated the adoption with a public feast. They gave gifts to the adoptee and his or her family and received gifts from them in return. The adoptee did not actually change his or her own clan membership but was symbolically rec-ognized as a member of the deceased's clan as well.

In her autobiography, the Fox woman recalled her sorrow after the death of her husband and described the mourning rituals of the Fox:

I cried in vain, as I felt so badly about him. Soon it was terrible for me. I undid my hair and loosened it. For several nights I could not sleep as I was sorrowful. On the fourth day I

Appanoose was a 19th-century peace chief of the Sac. Whites often misunderstood the roles of chiefs in Native American societies. With the Sac and Fox, as with other Native American peoples, such individuals led by force of personality and influence, not through any inherent power of the position to compel allegiance. Individuals were always free to make up their own minds regarding a chief's decision or policy.

called the men. "You are to divide all these possessions of ours among you," I said to my male relatives. And then the female relatives of my dead husband came to comb my hair. And they brought other garments for me to wear. I wore black clothing.

Then my mother's brother came and instructed me. "If you are sorry for your husband while still bound by death ceremonies, you would not go where something is going on," he said to me. "And do not talk much, and do not laugh. You must be merely always quietly making something. Nor must you look around too much."

When they are taken to be buried, those surviving accompany them. After they have spoken to the dead, the relatives of the dead begin to throw tobacco for them, then others afterward, then last of all the husbands or wives offer tobacco to them. They walk around in a circle where the dead is. Then they walk toward the East. They are never to look backward. If they were to look backward they would die soon.

The Sac and Fox both had systems of political leadership consisting of two different kinds of chiefs: civil or peace chiefs and war chiefs. Peace chiefs were men who had distinguished themselves throughout their lives. They were intelligent, generous, kind, and good tempered. People sought the chiefs' advice because they were reasonable, careful in their judgment, and helpful to others. A chief hoped to pass his position to one of his sons, but inheritance was not automatic. The son had to deserve the position of chief by virtue of his own success and his own personality and behavior.

Among the Sac, one chief was chosen from among all the others to be the "paramount" or most important leader. This man had to belong to the Sturgeon clan. Among the Fox, the leading peace chief had to be a member of the Bear clan.

All of the peace chiefs were important people in their communities, but they did not have absolute power. They could influence other people through their advice and counsel but they could not force anyone to obey their wishes or judgments. All tribespeople had the right to make up their own minds and do what they thought best.

Peace chiefs often met in councils to discuss important matters that arose in their communities. If individuals had disputes among themselves, they might take the issue to the council and ask for advice. Whenever the Sac or Fox negotiated alliances or treaties with other groups, the council discussed the agreements and evaluated the terms. When the chiefs reached a decision, they chose a man, or crier, to carry their message to each village and announce their decision. The council could also send a crier with messages for individuals who represented the Sac or Fox at meetings with foreign groups.

Although women were not named as chiefs and did not hold formal political office, they had a great deal of influence in their communities. They participated in public meetings and discussions. They made public speeches at such meetings, voiced their opinions, and gave their advice.

The Sac had two war chiefs. Sac war chiefs came from the two different divisions of black and white. These men planned, organized, and led war expeditions. They also planned the defense of their own communities when under attack by enemies.

Among the Fox, one war chief was chosen. He had to belong to the Fox clan. The war chief's duties included supervising a group of men who served as village police. The police made sure that people behaved in an orderly fashion. They were also sent to enforce decisions of the village council. If anyone disobeyed their instructions or disrupted public order, the police could destroy all of the property belonging to the offender.

Sac and Fox war chiefs were selected because of their courage and success in war. They recruited other men to join them on expeditions against the people's enemies. But, like the peace chiefs, war chiefs could not force anyone to follow their plans. Each Sac or Fox man decided for himself whether to join the raid. If he thought the plans and goals were good, he participated. But if he did not approve, he remained at home and attended to his other duties.

The Sac and Fox carried out raids against other groups for a variety of reasons. Vengeance was a common motive. If a member of one's family had been killed by someone from another tribe, the victim's relatives often led a raid against the murderer and his or her kin. If a murder was committed by a member of one's own group, the raids usually did not occur. In these cases, the relatives of the murderer offered valuable gifts to the victim's family in order to compensate for their loss. The victim's kin first refused the gifts, but eventually they accepted them so that peaceful community relations could be restored.

Sac and Fox men also organized raids to punish enemies who intruded on their hunting territories. In earlier times, such intrusions and raids were probably rare. But in later years, after European settlement caused many tribal relocations, warfare to protect one's territory became more frequent.

When a man wanted to plan a raid, he first built a small lodge outside his village. On the door to his lodge, he hung a strip of red cloth or a woven belt of red beads. When other men saw the lodge and the symbolic red belt, they knew the man's intentions. If they were interested in joining the raid, they went to the lodge, discussed the plans, and made their final preparations. In some cases, the wives of warriors joined their husbands on raids.

If warriors were successful in injuring or defeating their enemies, they returned to their territory and set up a camp outside their home village. Then they sent a man into the village to announce their arrival. The community prepared for a victory celebration and dance. When the warriors entered the village, they were promptly honored with feasting and dancing.

In some cases, Sac and Fox warriors brought back captives whom they had taken in raids. These captives, both men and women, were usually adopted by Sac or Fox families who had lost relatives in warfare. The Sac and Fox treated the adoptees like other members of their family.

The religious beliefs and practices of the Sac and Fox centered on a world of spirits that exercised direct influence on people's lives. The Sac and Fox believed in spirits of many kinds. According to their beliefs, the world was divided into two realms. The upper realm encompassed the sky and all celestial bodies. The lower realm consisted of the earth and the region under the earth. A spirit called the Great or Gentle Manitou lived in the sky. This spirit watched over the earth and all the creatures living on it.

Each of the four directions—east, west, north, and south—had important spirits associated with it. The spirit of the sun was linked to the East. A spirit named Wisahkeha lived in the North. He was credited with creating many kinds of animals and natural forms such as mountains and lakes. His younger brother, Kiyapahteha, resided in the West. He ruled over the souls of the dead who journeyed to the West when life ended. Finally, the spirit of Thunder lived in the South.

The Sac and Fox believed in many other spirits associated with the earth, with various animals, plants, and natural forces. Some spirits guarded specific locales, such as a mountain, a lake or river, or a cave. When a Sac or Fox individual entered one of these places, she or he thanked the spirit there for its protection. In 1907, the folklorist William Jones recorded a Fox tale that illustrated some of their beliefs about the world they inhabited:

> It is said that once a long time ago
> when it was winter and the first fall
> of snow was on the ground, three men

Catlin's depiction of what he called a "slave dance" of the Sac and Fox. Both the Sac and Fox often took prisoners in raids against other Native American peoples. Such captives might be used as hostages in future negotiations between nations. Often, they were accepted as members of the Sac or Fox community and were adopted by families as replacements for loved ones lost in battle or to illness.

went forth to hunt for game early in the morning. They came upon a place on the side of a hill where there was a thick growth of shrub. They saw the trail of a bear who had entered the spot. One of the men went in after the bear. The bear then ran away. Another man said: "Look, he is running away."

As the bear fled, the men chased after him. The bear led the men up into the sky. At first, the men did not notice that they were up in the sky. But then one man shouted, "Let us turn back. He is leading us into the sky." But the others did not answer him.

In the fall, the men overtook the bear and killed him. Then they cut off many boughs from an oak tree and put the bear's body on the branches. They cut the bear meat into pieces and

According to Catlin, this individual's name translated in English as "the Fire," and he was a Fox medicine man. Such individuals held influence in Sac and Fox society by virtue of their knowledge of medicinal plants and herbs and their understanding of the spirit world.

scattered the parts in all directions. They hurled the head toward the place where the dawn of day comes. That is why in the wintertime when dawn is nearly breaking, certain stars appear. It is said that the stars are the bear's head.

Then the hunters threw the bear's backbone toward the east. It is also common in wintertime for certain stars to be seen lying close together. It is said that they are the bear's backbone.

And it is told that the group of four stars in the sky is the bear and the three stars behind them are the hunters in pursuit of the bear.

And often in the autumn the leaves of oak trees turn red. That is because the hunters placed the bear's body on oak branches and his blood turned the leaves to red.

That is the end of the story.

Some spirits became personal guardians of individual people. A Sac or Fox man or woman could obtain such a guardian through a vision or dream. Upon reaching adulthood, she or he could begin to pray for the aid of a spirit helper. The spirit responded by giving the seeker a sign of its presence. Material objects such as an animal's tooth, a bird's feather, or a stone of unusual shape or appearance could serve as signs of the spirits. The vision seeker kept the object as a token of his or her guardian. Whenever the seeker was in danger or in need of help, she or he held it and prayed to the spirit that it represented. The spirit responded with a comforting message or instruction.

The Sac and Fox believed that spirits could appear to people in dreams in order to give warnings or advice. If someone was troubled by illness or misfortune, a spirit might offer a cure or solution. If someone had to make an important decision, a spirit might give advice on the proper course of action.

If an individual wanted to make contact with a spirit, there were a number of ways to give a signal to the supernatural realm. One blackened one's face with charcoal to show the spirits that their advice was wanted. The supplicant might fast in order to receive a vision from the spirit world. Or he or she might sing and wail to show the spirits his or her longing for contact with them. Finally, a seeker might offer burning tobacco to the spirits. The Sac and Fox believed that spirits understood these various signals and responded with advice, instructions, or other messages.

The spirit helpers and protectors gave the Sac and Fox a feeling of security and assurance that they were not alone. The people felt comfortable in the world they lived in, believing that they could depend upon spirit guardians when their own human abilities failed them.

But the Sac and Fox also depended upon each other in times of need. The belief that people should be generous, cooperative, and helpful to others informed all of their actions. They shared their goods and resources with relatives and neighbors, making sure that everyone had a decent life. The 19th-century Sac leader Black Hawk described these social ethics as follows:

Catlin's 1835 depiction of a massive Indian athletic contest. Many Native American peoples, including the Sac and Fox, played a variation of the ballgame known today as lacrosse. Their games sometimes involved hundreds of participants on a field that might be miles long.

We must continue throughout our lives to do what we conceive to be good. If we have corn and meat, and know of a family that have none, we divide with them. If we have more blankets than sufficient, and others have not enough, we must give to them that want.

The Sac and Fox recognized their responsibility to their community and expected cooperation from each other. When people had good fortune, such as the birth of a baby or a successful harvest, they invited relatives and neigh-bors to help celebrate. The hosts made feasts and shared their bounty with others.

The lives of the Sac and Fox consisted of yearly rounds of activities, including work, social events, and religious cere-monies. In the spring, the people gath-ered in their large permanent villages. The women planted the nearby fields with corn, pumpkins, beans, and squash. The men fished and hunted in the rivers and woods.

The summer months were times of plenty, as the crops ripened and the forests were filled with game. The people often held feasts to celebrate their good fortune. At the public celebrations, young people competed in sports, such as races and ball games like lacrosse, an original Native American sport that was widely enjoyed in eastern and midwestern North America. During the summer, the Sac and Fox visited their relatives and friends and renewed social bonds. Summer was also a season when young people met each other and might decide on a future marriage.

In the early fall, women harvested their last crops. Then village leaders selected a crier to announce the date of departure from the town. People began to prepare for the fall hunting season. Before leaving their villages, the Sac and Fox stored a quantity of dried corn, beans, and berries in their lodges and in containers buried in the ground so that when they returned the following spring they would have a supply of food ready to eat.

After making all necessary preparations, the Sac and Fox left their villages in small groups of related families. They set out on hunting expeditions. The members of each group traveled together from place to place and set up temporary camps. They built small lodges of bark, branches, and earth. The men left the camps in order to hunt for deer, elk, and buffalo. If the hunting was successful, the families remained in the same place for a while, but if the men were unable to catch animals in that locale, the people moved elsewhere and hoped for better results.

The hunting season lasted into the winter. During the colder winter months, the men hunted smaller game such as beaver and muskrat. Trapping of these animals continued well into the spring.

When spring approached, the people once again returned to their permanent lodges in the large villages. They repaired any damage to their homes caused by deterioration or bad weather. They took out the food that they had carefully stored the previous autumn. Then the women began their tasks of planting crops.

And so the yearly cycles of planting, harvesting, hunting, feasting, and celebrating continued, lending to the lives of the Sac and Fox a sense of permanence, security, and comfort. ▲

This tomahawk belonged to a member of a 19th-century eastern Indian tribe and was probably obtained in trade from whites, who manufactured it—note the scene depicted on the blade—to appeal to potential Native American customers.

CENTURIES
OF
CHANGE

For the Sac and the Fox, the 17th and 18th centuries were periods of change and adjustment. Both tribes relocated several times as they reacted to incursions into their territory by other native peoples and by Europeans. Despite these moves, the Sac and Fox succeeded in maintaining their traditional ways of living.

During the first half of the 17th century, the Sac and Fox left their ancestral lands in Michigan and resettled in the West. The Sac and Fox were in danger of raids by the Iroquois, whose home base was in New York State. The Iroquois waged war against neighboring peoples in order to dominate the fur trade between American Indians and British and French merchants. Trade between Native Americans and Europeans began in the 17th century and involved many native nations. When the supply of beaver in the New York area decreased because of overtrapping,

some Indians tried to establish themselves as middlemen between the Europeans and groups to the north and west. The Iroquois were by far the most successful in controlling trade. The military prowess of the Iroquois resulted in frequent tension and conflict in the Northeast.

These conditions convinced some American Indians to leave their own territory and seek refuge and security in western regions. But as they moved west, they often encroached on land already occupied by other peoples. Conflicts between original inhabitants and refugees led to additional migrations and relocations. This sequence of events was caused by the arrival of Europeans in North America. These newcomers hoped to profit from trade with native peoples. The Sac and Fox felt the direct and indirect results of this process.

As warfare intensified in the middle of the 17th century, the Sac and Fox were

Native Americans trade furs for goods at a British trading post. In the earliest days of white settlement, both whites and Indians often found it mutually beneficial to maintain amicable trade relations. Whites used Native Americans as the labor force that supplied them with the furs and animal skins they desired, in exchange for which Indians obtained the goods—particularly guns, metal tools and implements, and woven cloth—that they craved.

attacked by Iroquois warriors who ranged far north and west of their own territory. The Sac and Fox in Michigan also felt pressure from other Native Americans who migrated west as they fled from the intensifying conflict in the East. The Sac and Fox then left their territory in Michigan and headed northwest into northern Wisconsin. There they hoped to be safe from raids and from the migrations of other peoples.

Initially, the Sac and Fox were able to reestablish their lives in peace in northeastern Wisconsin. The Sac built their villages along the lower portion of the Fox River and around Green Bay, and the Fox settled along the upper Fox River and the Wolf River. The two groups resumed their traditional rounds of economic and social activities.

The Sac and Fox maintained friendly relations with most of their Indian neighbors in their new territory. These groups included the Kickapoo, Potawatomi, Winnebago, and Menomini.

During the second half of the 17th century, the Sac and Fox encountered French traders, explorers, and missionaries. The Sac and Fox often visited a French trading post at a place called Chequamegon on the southern shore of Lake Superior. Chequamegon was a center of trading activity for many other Indians from the upper Great Lakes region as well. French merchants and missionaries occasionally traveled to several Sac settlements in the vicinity of Green Bay. A French Jesuit priest, Father Allouez, visited the Sac at Green Bay and wrote that they were "very numerous."

The Sac and the Fox had quite different relations with the French. Throughout the latter years of the 17th century and the early part of the 18th, the Sac traded with French merchants in the region of the Great Lakes. The Sac traded animal skins, especially beaver, deer, and muskrat, to the French. In return, they obtained goods made of metal, including nails, knives, axes, and pots. Both the Sac and the French benefited from this trade. French merchants sold the fur for handsome profits in European markets. And the Sac valued the durable metal items that they received.

The Fox also wanted to obtain manufactured goods from the French. However, the two groups were not always on friendly terms. The Fox occasionally visited the French post at Chequamegon and another post established at Green Bay. But the Fox were soon angered by

the fact that the French traded with the Lakota (also known as the Sioux), a Native American people who were enemies of the Fox. The Lakota lived west of the Fox in the present-day states of North and South Dakota, Nebraska, and Wyoming. In order to visit French trading posts, the Lakota had to travel east through the region occupied by the Fox. When the Lakota crossed Fox territory, the two groups sometimes raided each other. The Fox blamed the French for continuing to trade with the Lakota. And the French blamed the Fox for causing trouble. As a result of tensions in the region, the French launched several attacks against the Fox in the early 18th century.

The Fox had additional troubles with the French and with Indian peoples in other locations. In 1710, the Fox established a village near the present-day city of Detroit in southeastern Michigan. There they traded with French merchants at a post known as Fort Pontchartrain. The Fox came into conflict with some other Indians who traded there. The Fox and their allies the Kickapoo tried to defend the Fox village against raids by other Indians, but the settlement near Detroit was destroyed in 1712. The survivors journeyed northwest and joined their tribespeople in Wisconsin.

During the same period, the Fox suffered further defeats at the hands of the French and the Wyandot, who were Indian allies of the French. After these losses, a group of Fox set out eastward to join the Seneca, one of the five nations of the Iroquois confederacy. They lived in western New York and northwestern Pennsylvania. The Fox crossed through the Ohio River valley south of Lake Erie. When they arrived in Seneca territory, they were welcomed by the people there. The Fox built a separate village for themselves in Seneca lands. They remained until 1779, when the settlement was destroyed by American soldiers during the American Revolution.

The French in Wisconsin continued to attack Fox settlements there. In 1716, the French army maintained a siege of a major Fox village for three days. Despite the siege, the Fox refused to surrender. The French soldiers finally withdrew to their fort.

In the late 1720s, the French again waged attacks against the Fox in Wisconsin. In response, the Fox tried to obtain support from other Native American groups in their conflict with the French. They hoped to unite the Winnebago and Kickapoo against the French. Although members of these groups did occasionally join Fox forces, as a whole they did not maintain a permanent alliance.

Because of increasing conflict and danger in the region, in 1730 a group of 300 Fox warriors and their families journeyed eastward to join the Fox contingent that was living among the Seneca. On the way, they came under attack by Indian allies of the French. Some of the Fox returned to Wisconsin, but most arrived safely in Seneca territory. The Fox built several villages and resided there from 1730 until 1791. The largest settlements were in southwestern New

York. A few smaller villages were established along the Allegheny River in northwestern Pennsylvania. The Seneca welcomed the Fox refugees, because the Fox villages acted as buffers between the Seneca and European colonists living in neighboring areas.

For their part, the Sac wanted to maintain good relations with the French, but they also valued their traditional alliance with the Fox. When intense warfare erupted between the Fox and the French in the early 1700s, the Sac followed an official policy of neutrality. However, they actually aided the Fox. Then, in 1733, the French launched several attacks against the Fox with the intention of destroying all of their villages and permanently driving them away. Many of the Fox took refuge among the Sac. The French commander, Nicolas-Antoine Coulon de Villiers, demanded that the Sac surrender the Fox refugees. The Sac chiefs refused. In retaliation, Villiers attacked both the Sac and Fox. Although the Indians defeated the French forces, they decided to leave the region and seek safety and stability elsewhere. They traveled south into present-day Iowa and Illinois, where many settled along the Mississippi and Rock rivers.

Relations between the Sac and the French soon improved. In 1737, the two nations declared their mutual friendship. French merchants, who wanted to resume their profitable trade relations with the Sac, then persuaded some of the Sac to return to Wisconsin. The French also offered peace to the Fox in

A skirmish between Lakota (also known as Sioux) and Sac and Fox warriors, as depicted by Catlin in the late 1840s. The Sac and Fox and the Lakota were frequently at war, largely because the Lakota feared the Sac and Fox would displace them as trading partners with European and American merchants.

1743. In that year, the Fox returned to the area near the Fox River in Wisconsin to trade with French merchants.

But by 1766, the Sac and Fox had left Wisconsin, settling once again in villages near the Mississippi, Rock, and Wisconsin rivers. The Sac built their large vil-

lage of Saukenuk, containing some 100 lodges, at the junction of the Rock and the Mississippi. The largest settlement of the Fox held approximately 50 lodges.

Once established in Illinois and Iowa, the Sac and Fox encountered, in trade and warfare, other Native American

By the late 18th century, two kinds of forts had begun to appear near or on Sac and Fox territory. These were strongholds erected and inhabited by soldiers or militia for the protection of settlers, as well as fortified commercial outposts maintained by fur-trading concerns for the conducting of business.

peoples who resided in the region. Most of their relationships were friendly, but the Sac and Fox made enemies of some nearby nations, including the Osage, Illinois, Cherokee, and Chippewa. Conflict between the Sac and the Osage was frequent. And the Fox often carried out raids against the Illinois and Chippewa.

In their new territory, the Sac and Fox met European traders from Spain. The Spanish built trading posts along the Mississippi River and attracted business from many Indians, including the Sac and Fox. A large Spanish post was located at St. Louis. There the Sac and Fox traded animal furs and farm produce for European manufactured goods. By the latter half of the 18th century, the Sac and Fox had also obtained a steady supply of horses from Spanish traders. Although species of horses had lived in North America in prehistoric times, they had become extinct long before human beings arrived on the continent. Modern horses were brought to North America by Spanish conquistadores in the 16th century. Many Indians began to acquire horses at that time.

The Sac and Fox made good use of the horses they obtained. Like other

Indian peoples in the prairie and Plains regions of North America, the Sac and Fox prized horses highly because they provided an excellent means of transportation. Once hunters were able to ride on horseback, they could travel much longer distances than when they had to walk. Horses also could carry hides and meat from the hunting territory to the Sac and Fox villages.

In addition to obtaining goods from French and Spanish merchants, the Sac and Fox traded with the British. The British built many posts near the Great Lakes in Canada and along the Mississippi River. The Sac and Fox maintained

A British soldier bayonets an Indian ally of his French enemy during the French and Indian War, which the two European nations fought between 1756 and 1763 on North American soil for control of the continent. As much as was possible, the Sac and Fox sought to avoid taking sides in the contest.

During the American Revolution, as during the French and Indian War, both sides sought to enlist Native Americans to their cause. This rather grisly 19th-century illustration depicts the massacre of American settlers in the Wyoming River valley of Pennsylvania by Native American forces allied with the British. Unlike their frequent enemies the Iroquois, the Sac and Fox did not play a significant role in the fighting during the American Revolution, although they suffered greatly as a result of the conflict.

good trade relations with all the European merchants in their new region.

By the middle of the 18th century, the traditional rivalry between the British and the French was playing itself out in the New World. From 1756 to 1763, this hostility was enacted in an all-out war for control of North America. The two European nations tried to involve their Indian trading partners as allies in the conflict. Since the Sac and Fox traded with both Britain and France, they were reluctant to take sides in the French and

Indian War. Some favored the British and others the French, but most of the Sac and Fox remained neutral.

After the war, the Sac and Fox resumed their peaceful relations with the victorious British. But they also continued to trade with French merchants who had by then moved their posts to territory controlled by Spain in the Midwest.

A few years later, in 1776, the American War of Independence erupted. The Sac and Fox became involved in the conflict. Both the Americans and the British tried to obtain support from the Indians, but the Sac and Fox were divided in their allegiance. Some sided with the colonists, others with the British, and still others remained neutral. The American colonists offered the Sac and Fox good trade terms in return for their help. At the same time, the British promised to protect the territory of the Sac and Fox from intrusions by American settlers. By the time of the revolutionary war, many settlers had invaded the Indians' land. Some Sac and Fox sided with the British because they feared further encroachments by the Americans.

Despite pleas for support from the British and the colonists, most of the Sac and Fox remained neutral during the War of Independence. However, in 1780, some Sac and Fox warriors joined British soldiers in assaults against colonial forces in St. Louis and in Cahokia, Illinois. In retaliation, American forces attacked several Sac settlements near the Rock River, even though the victims of the raids had not taken part in the British campaign. In fact, the Sac living at Rock River were actually on the side of the Americans. The Americans burned Sac villages, killed many inhabitants, and destroyed their farms. The survivors quickly fled from the area. In reaction to the attacks, all of the Sac and Fox turned against the colonists and threw their support to the British. After the war ended, the Sac and Fox refused to sign a peace treaty with the Americans.

By the close of the 18th century, peace had returned to the region occupied by the Sac and Fox. The people again engaged in their traditional activities. The women planted and harvested their crops. The men hunted and fished. And all celebrated their good fortune. But the lands of the Sac and Fox were soon invaded by increasing numbers of American settlers. The Indians' lives were disrupted once again. ▲

An Indian leader orates at the 1794 negotiations that resulted in
the Treaty of Greenville the following year. The treaty brought
to an end, for a time, hostilities between Native Americans and the
new nation of the United States in the Old Northwest Territory,
which lay between the Ohio and Mississippi rivers and was
homeland to, among others, the Sac and Fox.

THE
CRITICAL
YEARS

Following the War of Independence, American settlers resumed their westward migration, and the expansion of the new United States encroached on the lands of many tribes of Native Americans. The Sac and Fox were among the many tribes whose territory was invaded.

The early years of the 19th century was a time of rapid growth in the size and power of the newly formed United States. In 1800, the U.S. Congress created the Indiana Territory from land west of the original 13 American states. Indiana stretched from the Ohio River north to the border with Canada and extended west to the Mississippi River. At that time, some 5,500 American settlers resided in Indiana Territory. Thousands of Native Americans lived there as well, including 4,000 or 5,000 Sac and 2,000 or 3,000 Fox.

In 1803, the United States greatly expanded its territory by purchasing the Louisiana Territory from France. Louisiana consisted of a huge expanse of land west of the Mississippi River that stretched north from the Gulf of Mexico almost to the Canadian border and west to the Rocky Mountains. President Thomas Jefferson wanted the United States to obtain title to land held by Indians living in Louisiana. He and his government began to pressure native peoples to sell their land and resettle in designated territories elsewhere.

During the first half of the 19th century, the Sac and Fox faced the choice of resisting the intruders or abandoning their homeland. Sometimes they chose to resist, and at other times they agreed to leave their lands and relocate farther west. When the Sac and Fox resisted the settlers' advance, conflicts and warfare often erupted. The U.S. government promoted the settlers' cause by supporting their claims to Indian land. And when conflicts arose, officials sided with the settlers.

But the government preferred to avoid open warfare. Instead, they tried to convince the Sac, Fox, and other Indians to sign treaties that relinquished their territory. The Sac and Fox at first refused to agree to such treaties. In response to their resistance, the government used a number of methods to pressure them to come to terms.

First, the government built forts and military posts along the Mississippi River near the territory of the Sac and Fox. In 1808, the army built the first of a series of forts in the region. Named Fort Madison, after the president at the time, it was located north of the present-day city of Des Moines, Iowa. Although the Sac and Fox objected to the presence of soldiers so close to their villages, the army refused to leave.

Second, the government tried to convince the Sac and Fox to give up their land in exchange for forgiveness of debts that the Indians owed to American traders. As President Thomas Jefferson explained in 1803:

> We observe that when these debts get beyond what the individuals can pay, they become willing to lop them off by a cession of lands.

And third, the government encouraged the Sac and Fox to sign treaties without fully explaining the terms. Since most Sac and Fox did not understand English, they had to rely on translators who did not always report the significance of the words in the treaties. After signing the agreements, the Sac and Fox were forced to follow the terms of the treaties, even if they did not fully understand them.

Beginning in the first few years of the 19th century, the government tried to persuade the Sac and Fox to give up a portion of their territory in Illinois east of the Mississippi River. The Indians repeatedly refused to move. Then, in 1804, four Sac representatives met with William Henry Harrison, governor of the Illinois and Indiana territories, to discuss their situation. The representatives agreed to sign a treaty that ceded the territory of the Sac and Fox lying east of the Mississippi.

The meeting of 1804 was preceded by a series of confusing events. The problem began when two Sacs, along with a group of Indians from other nations, became involved in skirmishes with American settlers in which several settlers were killed. The U.S. government wanted to punish the Indians who were responsible for the settlers' deaths. In an effort to restore peace, Sac chiefs held a council and decided to meet with the Americans and negotiate a settlement. They sent a delegation of four representatives to meet with Governor Harrison in St. Louis. According to the system of justice of the Sac and Fox, when someone commits a murder, his relatives offer payment to relatives of the deceased as atonement for the crime.

In this 19th-century engraving, Thomas Jefferson signs the papers that commit the United States to the purchase of the Louisiana Territory, a vast tract between the Mississippi River and Rocky Mountains from which all or part of 15 states would ultimately be carved.

But when the Sac delegates suggested compensation to Harrison, the governor rejected their offer. Instead, Harrison insisted that the Sac and Fox pay for the settlers' deaths with some of their land. The Sac delegates finally agreed to Harrison's demand.

The Sac thus lost the rights to their land east of the Mississippi in the present-day states of Illinois, Wisconsin, and Missouri. In exchange, the government promised a yearly payment, or annuity, for an unspecified period of time. The Sac were to receive $600 each year while the Fox were promised the sum of $400. The four Sac delegates who signed the treaty received gifts from the government of clothing and medals valued at $2,234.50. By the terms of the treaty, the Sac and Fox were permitted to remain in their territory as long as the U.S. government held the land. But if and when the government sold the land to individual settlers, the Sac and Fox would be forced to leave.

When the Sac and Fox discovered the true terms of the Treaty of 1804, they were stunned and angry. The chiefs said that the treaty was unjust. And they insisted that the four Sac signers did not have the authority to sell the people's land.

When the Sac delegates returned to their village, they wore the coats and medals that Harrison had given them. And they appeared to have been drinking heavily. Sac leaders believed that Harrison had deliberately gotten the delegates drunk and had given them personal gifts of clothing as bribes for signing the treaty.

In the following years, increasing numbers of settlers streamed into the territory of the Sac and Fox. During this period, the Sac and Fox continued to live in their traditional villages. A census taken in 1805 reported that 2,850 Sac resided in three villages. The census listed 700 men, 750 women, and 1,400 children. The Fox also occupied three villages at the time. Their population of 1,750 people included 400 men, 500 women, and 850 children.

Conflicts between the Indians and the settlers intensified throughout the early 19th century. Tensions mounted steadily and casualties occurred on both sides. As more settlers poured into Sac and Fox lands, the chiefs appealed to American officials for protection. But local authorities did nothing to help the Indians.

Then, in January 1806, seven Sac delegates traveled to Washington, D.C., to speak with President Jefferson about the settlers' incursions into their territory. Jefferson told them: "Our nation is numerous and strong; but we wish to be just to all; and particularly to be kind and useful to all our red children."

Despite these friendly words, Jefferson took no action to stop settlers from encroaching on Sac and Fox land. Even when Sac and Fox men and women were killed by American intruders, the government did not punish the wrongdoers. Indeed, the presence of Fort Madison in the heart of the region protected the settlers and intimidated the Sac and Fox.

During the same period, the U.S. government tried to discourage the Sac and Fox from trading with British mer-

As governor of the Indiana Territory, William Henry Harrison led the U.S. forces that defeated the Indian confederacy headed by Tecumseh at the Battle of Tippecanoe in 1811. That victory, and the subsequent U.S. triumph in the War of 1812, which rid the Old Northwest of British influence, led to a new influx of American settlement in Sac and Fox territory.

American forces (at left, in the stockade) hold off an attack by British troops and their Indian allies during the War of 1812. The war was caused, in part, by the continued presence of the British in the Old Northwest, where the U.S. government believed they were constantly engaged in fomenting unrest among the Native American peoples who lived there.

chants. The government wanted the Indians to trade only with Americans. But the Sac and Fox continued to trade at British posts in Malden and Amherstburg in Ontario, Canada. There the British merchants gave the Sac and Fox personal gifts as well as trade goods.

The Sac and Fox traded with American merchants as well, which was profitable for both sides. In fact, in 1806, the American explorers Meriwether Lewis and William Clark estimated that American merchants received furs from the Indians worth $10,000 per year.

Despite good trade relations, hostility toward the Americans increased because of the continual encroachment of American settlers on Indian territory. In 1810, a Shawnee leader named Tecumseh tried to unite Native Americans from numerous nations against the settlers who continued to pour into the Midwest. Tecumseh sent messengers to the Sac and Fox asking them to meet with him. The Sac leader, Black Hawk, reported Tecumseh's warning:

> He explained to us the bad treatment the different nations of Indians had received from the Americans, by giving them a few presents, and taking their land from them. I

remember well his saying: "If you do not join your friends, the Americans will take this very village from you!" I little thought then, that his words would come true!

The Sac and Fox did not join Tecumseh's forces. But when Tecumseh's early clashes with Americans proved successful, a number of Sac and Fox attacked the American army unit at Fort Madison. Since the fort was well protected, the Indians were unable to accomplish their goal. Tecumseh's plan to unite Indians in the Mississippi and Great Lakes regions failed. Although he gained many followers from several nations, he could not convince the majority to join him.

During the same period, tensions between the United States and Great Britain increased. The conflict erupted into the War of 1812. Among the causes, the Americans resented what they considered to be British interference with Indians in the United States. Americans did not want the British in Canada to trade with Indians, including the Sac and Fox, who resided in the United States. In order to stop the ongoing trade, the American government made it illegal to import British goods into the United States.

But the Sac and Fox still traded with both British and American merchants. Although American posts were nearby, the Sac and Fox preferred to deal with British traders because the British gave a better price in goods for the furs brought by the Indians. British merchants also gave the Sac and Fox personal presents of clothing, food, guns, and ammunition.

In addition to favorable terms and generous presents, British merchants extended credit to the Sac and Fox. Since the Indians' hunting expeditions took place in the fall and winter, they depended on credit during the spring and summer. After their hunting and trapping season ended, they paid their debts and renewed the cycle of credit and payment.

When the War of 1812 began, the British sought support from the Sac and Fox. The Americans hoped that the Sac and Fox would at least remain neutral. In 1813, President James Madison invited a delegation of Sac and Fox chiefs to meet with him in Washington, D.C. He advised them not to trust the British and added:

> I say to you, my children, your father does not ask you to join his warriors. Sit still on your seats and be witnesses that they are able to beat their enemies and protect their red friends.

Encouraged by Madison's words, the Sac and Fox asked the president to persuade American merchants to extend credit to them at the posts. Madison agreed to do so, but when Sac and Fox hunters next went to the American trading post at Fort Madison, the merchant there refused to give them credit. When the Indians told him of President Madison's promise, the trader still refused the

The Sac leader Keokuk, whose Indian name translates as Running Fox, recognized the inevitable and led his followers across the Mississippi River into Iowa in 1829.

credit. The Sac and Fox felt that Madison had betrayed them. Shortly afterward, they received a boatload of gifts from British traders who had posts near Detroit and Prairie du Chien. The Sac and Fox then resumed trading with the British. As a result of the Americans' refusal to give credit and of the generosity of the British, some Sac and Fox decided to aid the British in the War of 1812.

In an effort to obtain military support from the Indians, Robert Dixon, a colonel in the British army, asked the Sac war chief Black Hawk to meet with him. Dixon conferred the rank of general on Black Hawk and told him:

> You will now have to hold us fast by the hand. Your English father [the King] has found out that the Americans want to take your country from you—and has sent me and his braves to drive them back to their own country. He has sent a large quantity of arms and ammunition— and we want all your warriors to join us.

Five hundred Sac warriors set out in January of 1813 to join the British forces in Detroit. They attacked several American forts in the region. The assaults were indecisive, with both sides suffering numerous casualties.

Although some Sac and Fox warriors aided the British, others favored the Americans during the war. In 1813, a group of Sac who were sympathetic to the Americans left Illinois and moved west of the Mississippi River. They established villages in Missouri under the protection of the U.S. government.

In 1816, British authorities informed their Sac and Fox allies that the war between Great Britain and the United States had ended. Sac chiefs then received an invitation from U.S. general William Clark, governor of Missouri Territory, to meet with him in St. Louis. Several civil chiefs went to St. Louis to confer with Clark.

Clark immediately accused the Sac of betraying the Americans during the war with Great Britain. The chiefs justi-

continued on page 65

USEFUL BEAUTY

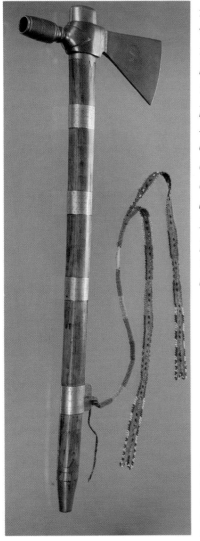

Pictured in this section are several representative items of Sac and Fox material culture. These objects include toys, weapons, household items, garments, and personal adornments; each has in common with the other that it has both a practical use and a greater significance, one that symbolizes, for example, its owner's status in Sac and Fox society or serves as a reminder to the members of the nation of eternal truths about the world they inhabit. Before the advent of whites in the Sac and Fox homeland, such objects would have been fashioned from the raw materials of their environment—animal skins, parts, and dyes; plant and natural fibers; wood and stone. Afterwards, the people used materials that they obtained in trade from whites—most notably colored beads, metal goods, and woven cloth—to craft the items they needed. White manufacturers also made goods specifically for trade with the Indians, such as the tomahawk shown on this page. Despite such outside influence, Sac and Fox material culture continued to reflect the practical and spiritual concerns of its people.

This pipe tomahawk was manufactured by whites in the mid-19th century for trade with the Indians. The head was made of brass, the bands of pewter, and the handle of wood, which could be branded by the owner with individual designs.

58

On these pages are bandolier bags, which would be worn over the shoulder and might be used to carry powder, ammunition, tobacco, or religious charms. The bags were made of wool and cotton cloth, glass beads, silk ribbon, and yarn. The various designs probably depicted forces, spirits, or powers from the natural world, such as those controlling the winds, the seasons, or various animals.

These bags illustrate the way in which form and beauty was integrated in Sac and Fox material culture. The trunk at lower left was made from rawhide and pigment, while the two storage bags displayed were crafted from wool yarn, nettle fiber, and buckskin.

This headdress was known as a roach and was a special mark of status for Sac and Fox
warriors. Most often, such roaches were fashioned from hair taken from the tail of a deer
and eagle's feathers. The roach was affixed to a small tuft of hair on the crest of a warrior's
head, which was otherwise shaved virtually bald.

Made of otter skin and a bear claw, this headdress was also worn by Sac and Fox warriors and was considered a status symbol.

The body and feathers of a bird were used to make this fan.

continued from page 56

fied their actions by saying that President Madison had deceived them. Clark then told the chiefs that he "would break off the treaty and go to war" if the chiefs insulted him. The chiefs responded that they were simply explaining their actions.

At the end of the meeting, the Sac leaders signed a new treaty. The chiefs thought that they were signing a treaty of peace and friendship. They did not realize that the document also confirmed the terms of the Treaty of 1804, which gave away Sac and Fox territory. Without their understanding, they pledged to cede their lands east of the Mississippi River to the United States. The Sac thus joined the Fox in confirming the Treaty of 1804, for Fox chiefs had signed a similar statement of agreement in 1815.

When the Sac chiefs returned to their villages following the meeting with Governor Clark, they discovered that the American army was building a new fort, named Fort Armstrong, on Rock Island near the site of the Sac's principal village of Saukenuk. The Sac strongly objected to the presence of the fort in the midst of their own territory. But the American government ignored the Sac's objections.

The government also ignored the complaints of the Sac and Fox about the stream of American settlers who moved into their territory. As more Americans encroached on Sac and Fox lands, the people's hostility toward the settlers increased. At the same time, British officials gave promises of support to the Sac and Fox who traded at British posts in

For more than 20 years until his death at the Battle of the Thames in 1813, the Shawnee leader Tecumseh would be the most feared Indian opponent of the U.S. government. Tecumseh's goal was to forge an alliance of the Native American peoples of the Old Northwest. By 1808, according to the historian Samuel Eliot Morison, his influence "extended as far south as Florida, and northwest to Saskatchewan."

In 1803, Meriwether Lewis (left) and William Clark (right) were commissioned by President Thomas Jefferson to survey the Louisiana Territory, fashion a land route to the Pacific, and strengthen U.S. claims to the Pacific Northwest. Before their departure, the Sac and Fox regularly came to trade with the men of the Lewis and Clark expedition at their encampment near the confluence of the Missouri and Mississippi rivers. As the U.S. superintendent of Indian affairs, Clark would have a long subsequent history with the Sac and Fox.

Canada. The American government resented the fact that the Sac and Fox still traded with the British. But at least one American official recognized the root of the problem. Henry Schoolcraft, a U.S. agent to the Indians, wrote to his superiors in Washington:

> The causes of this increasing intercourse [with the British] are to be found not so much in any increased efforts of the British agents to alienate these bands from our government, as in the necessitous and impoverished state of the Indians.

Schoolcraft's reasonable words were largely ignored by his government.

At the same time that American settlers invaded Sac and Fox land in greater numbers, the population of the Sac and Fox was increasing. By 1820, a government census reported that the population of the Sac was between 4,000 and 5,000. The Fox numbered some 3,500.

In addition to their problems with American settlers and the United States government, the Sac and Fox faced increasing conflict with Indians in their region. As Sac and Fox hunters traveled north and west to hunt the huge herds of buffalo, they again came in contact with the Lakota. The Lakota objected to the intrusion of the Sac and Fox into their own hunting area. But the Sac and Fox were forced to hunt in the west because American settlers had taken over much of their own land. Clashes among the Indians were indirect results of the displacement of native peoples from their homelands as American settlers occupied the region.

As in past periods, the United States government did not stop the settlers' advances into Sac and Fox territory. Instead they appealed to the Indian nations to stop fighting with each other so that settlers would be able to move in and live in Indian territory without fear of warfare.

As the tensions increased, the American government tried to convince the Sac and Fox to sell more of their land. In 1824, a delegation of Sac and Fox leaders went to Washington and signed an agreement that ceded a tract of their territory west of the Mississippi River as far as Des Moines. In return, the United States paid them a sum of $1,000 and promised an additional annuity of $500 for a period of 10 years.

But the conflicts continued as more settlers moved onto land still held by the Sac and Fox. The Indians often complained to officials about assaults committed by settlers against native women and men. In his famous autobiography, Black Hawk recounted several such incidents:

> At one time, a white man beat one of
> our women cruelly, for pulling a
> few suckers of corn out of his field, to
> suck, when she was hungry. At
> another time, one of our young men

was beat with clubs by two white men for opening a fence which crossed our road, to take his horse through. His shoulder blade was broken, and his body badly bruised, from which he soon after died.

The U.S. government responded by exerting pressure on the Sac and Fox to sell all of their land east of the Mississippi River. In May 1828, Thomas Forsyth, the United States agent for the region, ordered the Sac and Fox to move from their villages in Illinois by the following spring. In the winter of 1829, the government put up for sale all of the Indians' territory covered by the Treaty of 1804.

Nearly all of the Fox decided to move west of the Mississippi into Iowa. Many of the Sac also agreed to relocate there. This group was led by a Sac man named Keokuk. He and his followers left Saukenuk after the summer harvest of 1829. But some Sac refused to abandon their homeland and vowed to remain in Saukenuk. In their view,

> Land cannot be sold. The Great Spirit
> gave it to his children to live upon,
> and cultivate, as far as is necessary for
> their subsistence; and so long as
> they occupy and cultivate it, they have
> the right to the soil.

But in the opinion of the U.S. government, of course, land *can* be bought and sold. And they had bought the Sac's land. Confrontation between the two peoples was inevitable. ▲

Bear's Track, who was painted by Catlin in the late 1830s, may have been among the Sac and Fox warriors who struck fear into the hearts of the white settlers of Illinois in 1832 when they crossed the Mississippi River under the leadership of Black Hawk.

WAR
ON
THE
FRONTIER

When the Sac returned to Saukenuk in the spring of 1830 after their fall and winter hunting expeditions, they found that American settlers were living in their village. American families had occupied the Sac's lodges and planted crops in the Sac's cornfields.

The Sac protested to Forsyth and demanded that he tell the settlers to leave the Sac's homes and fields. For their part, the settlers wanted Forsyth to force the Sac to leave the area. Black Hawk described the dispute:

> We acquainted our agent daily with our situation and hoped that something would be done for us. The whites were complaining at the same time that *we* were *intruding* upon *their rights! They* made themselves out the *injured* party, and *we* the *intruders* and called loudly to the great war chief to protect *their* property! How smooth must be the language of the whites, when they can make right look like wrong, and wrong like right.

Forsyth sided with the settlers. He urged the U.S. government to act swiftly to remove the Sac from Saukenuk.

As the crisis worsened for the Sac, a law enacted by the U.S. Congress in 1830 affected the controversy. Under the leadership of President Andrew Jackson, the Indian Removal Act was passed. This legislation ordered the forcible removal of many Indian nations living east of the Mississippi River to land west of the Mississippi. Although the law did not specifically mention the Sac, it was applied to their situation.

The Sac and their Fox allies were assigned to territory in present-day Iowa and Missouri. A majority of the people agreed to relocate there because they hoped that they could thereby avoid war

John Reynolds, governor of Illinois, lost little time in calling for the formation of a volunteer militia to repel Black Hawk's "invasion." One newspaper in the state called for "a war of extermination until there shall be no Indian . . . left in Illinois."

with the American settlers, who by then numbered more than 150,000 in Illinois.

Despite the resettlement of the Fox and most of the Sac, some Sac refused to move. Under Black Hawk's leadership, they sought assistance from other Indian groups, including their allies the Winnebago and Potawatomi. Leaders of these peoples offered support and encouragement. British officials and traders in Canada also gave promises of aid.

Armed with these pledges of support, Black Hawk and his followers returned to Saukenuk in the spring of 1831. The group numbered nearly 500 men, women, and children. In response to the Sac's return, John Reynolds, governor of Illinois, stated that the Sac's action was an "invasion of the United States." He called out a militia of 700 men to force the Sac to leave. He said that Sac men and women should be removed "dead or alive."

General Edmund Gaines, commander of the army's western division, also ordered the Sac to quit their homeland. Gaines called the Sac chiefs to a meeting on June 5, 1831. There he told the chiefs that they must comply with the terms of the treaties of 1804 and 1816, which ended the rights of the Sac and Fox to land east of the Mississippi River.

When Black Hawk told Gaines that the people intended to remain in their village, the general responded with a final warning:

> I came here neither to beg nor hire you to leave your village. My business is to remove you, peaceably if I can, but forcibly if I must! I will now give you two days to remove in— and if you do not cross the Mississippi within that time, I will adopt measures to force you away!

Shortly after the meeting ended, Keokuk, the leader of the Sac in Iowa, spoke with those who remained at Saukenuk. He urged them to stop opposing the American government. He argued that it was best to resettle west of the Mississippi. Keokuk was able to persuade most of the Sac to leave their homes and relocate to Iowa. But others still remained at Saukenuk.

After Gaines's meeting with the Sac, American officials and military leaders prepared a campaign against the people at Saukenuk. Toward the end of June 1831, General Gaines sent a militia of 1,400 men to the region. On June 25, the soldiers destroyed the Sac's fields and fired their guns at the village. None of the people were injured because they had hurriedly left the night before the assault. They took refuge across the Mississippi River and waited for the promised support from their allies among the Winnebago. The assistance never came.

Black Hawk then received a message from Gaines asking him to appear at another meeting. Since Black Hawk had no support from the British or from Indian allies, he decided to meet with Gaines and negotiate a peaceful resolution to the crisis.

At the meeting, Sac leaders signed a new treaty and promised to leave Saukenuk forever. The Sac also pledged to break off trade relations with British merchants in Canada. Finally, they agreed to follow the leadership of Keokuk in Iowa.

But despite the Sac's best intentions, their conflict with the United States government did not end. Several factors contributed to renewing the controversy. One factor was a resurgence of intertribal tensions in the region. In the first of a series of related events, several Fox chiefs were killed by Lakota and Menomini warriors. Fox warriors then avenged their chiefs' deaths by attacking a Menomini village in Illinois. As the U.S. government planned to send a military force against the Fox in response, the Fox asked for support from their Sac allies. Black Hawk responded favorably to their request because he believed that the U.S. government had no right to interfere in intertribal disputes.

A second factor in the continuing crisis between the Sac and the United States was a repeated promise of aid given to the Sac by British officials in Canada.

And third, a Winnebago leader named Wabokieshiek (White Cloud) assured the Sac that people from his own nation were willing to support the Sac's cause. He reported that the Sac could depend upon aid from the Potawatomi, Chippewa, and Ottawa as well.

These promises of support encouraged the Sac who wanted to return to Saukenuk. Some 600 warriors and their families decided to reclaim their homes in the spring of 1832.

When Keokuk heard of the Sac's plans to return to Saukenuk, he sent a message to American officials telling them of the Sac's decision. In response, General Henry Atkinson, commander of the U.S. Army in the region, sent a force of over 200 soldiers to Rock Island to prevent the Sac from crossing east of the Mississippi River. But by then, the Sac, numbering more than 2,000, had already crossed the Mississippi and were heading toward Saukenuk.

Atkinson next appealed for reinforcements from John Reynolds, governor of Illinois. Reynolds issued a call to American settlers to volunteer in defense of their towns. He claimed that the Americans were in "imminent danger" from the Sac, even though the Sac had never attacked innocent settlers. In answer to Reynolds's call, more than 1,700 settlers volunteered. They proceeded to Rock Island, where they met General Atkinson's troops on May 7, 1832.

While the American officers were gathering their forces, the Sac again received promises of aid from the Winnebago, the Potawatomi, and the British. But no support arrived.

The Sac soon ran out of provisions and renounced their intention of returning to Saukenuk. They headed west toward Iowa, walking through the woods to reach safety. Without adequate food and supplies, they subsisted on wild roots, grasses, and bark from trees.

Just as the Sac were quitting their territory, General Atkinson, General Samuel Whiteside, and Major Isaiah Stillman were massing their forces to attack them. Whiteside first found a

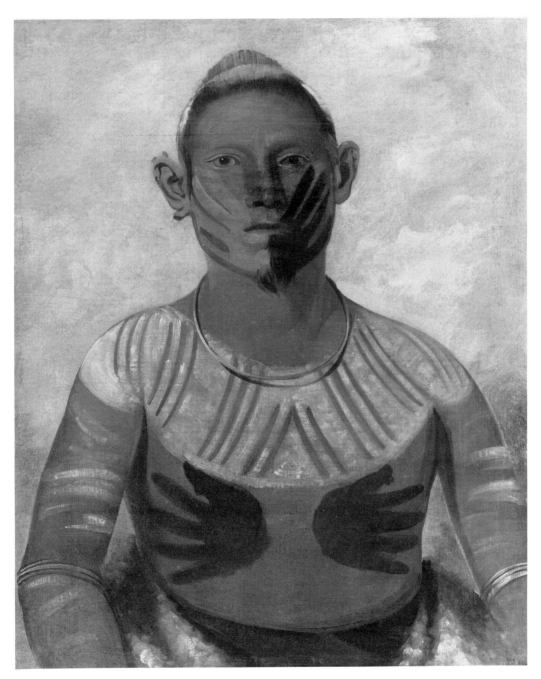

Ioway was one of Black Hawk's most trusted warriors. He sat for this portrait by Catlin in 1832.

Winnebago village where the Sac had taken a brief rest. Even though the Sac had already departed, Whiteside punished the Winnebago by burning their entire village.

Taking another route, General Stillman's troops followed the Sac along the Rock River west of the Mississippi. When Black Hawk learned that Stillman was near, he decided to surrender. He sent eight Sac men to meet Stillman with a white flag of peace. When the American force, consisting of volunteers, saw the Sac approach, they panicked and began firing at the Indians. Four of the eight Sac warriors were killed. The others escaped with their lives.

Then some 40 Sac warriors waited in ambush as the Americans neared their camp. They attacked the soldiers, killing some and frightening the rest. The soldiers hastily retreated to their base camp. In the alarm and confusion that followed, reports of the number of Sac warriors were grossly exaggerated. In this climate of tension and fear, Governor Reynolds issued a new appeal for volunteers. Two thousand men responded and joined the American forces.

As the crisis worsened, American settlers in Illinois grew increasingly alarmed. Government and military officials contributed to the deepening tension. One assistant to General Atkinson wrote:

> The alarm and distress on the frontier cannot be described. It is heartrending to see the women and

children in an agony of fear, fleeing from their homes and hearths, to seek what they imagine is but a brief respite from death.

When President Andrew Jackson learned of the crisis, he ordered his military officers to capture Black Hawk and his followers. Jackson blamed the Indians for causing trouble. In a letter to his secretary of war, John Robb, Jackson wrote:

> Black Hawk and his party must be chastized and a speedy and honorable termination put to this war, which will hereafter deter others from the like unprovoked hostilities by Indians on our frontier.

The Sac continued their trek westward along the Wisconsin River as they headed to Iowa. They hoped that if they returned to Iowa, they would be left alone to live in peace.

However, President Jackson ordered the American army to pursue and attack the Sac. On July 21, 1832, General James Dodge saw the Sac crossing an island in the Wisconsin River. Sac warriors managed to hold off the Americans while the women, children, and elderly crossed to temporary safety. But after the people reached the shore, they were attacked by another group of soldiers. The soldiers killed at least 70 Sac men, women, and children and took others prisoner. The surviving Sacs fled into the nearby woods.

By this time, the Sac were suffering from lack of adequate food and clothing.

General Joseph Street noted the sad condition of the Sac he had seen:

> The prisoners are the most miserable looking poor creatures you can imagine. Wasted to mere skeletons, clothed in rags scarcely sufficient to hide their nakedness, some of the children look as if they had starved so long they could not be restored.

On August 1, Black Hawk tried once again to surrender to American forces. As the Sac were crossing the Wisconsin River toward Iowa, Black Hawk saw a steamboat loaded with soldiers. He raised a white flag of peace and sent one of his men to offer surrender to the boat's captain. But the captain, Lieutenant Throckmorton, misunderstood the message. He thought that Black Hawk wanted the soldiers to surrender and come ashore.

Throckmorton then ordered an attack against the Sac. Nearly 30 of the Sac were killed in a heavy barrage of gunfire. The survivors fled into the woods to save themselves.

Meanwhile, General Atkinson was continuing his search for the Sac. Two days later, on August 3, 1832, Atkinson found the Sac crossing the Bad Axe River where it joined the Mississippi. He launched a full attack against the people. During more than eight hours of gunfire, some 200 men, women, and children were slaughtered indiscriminately. Black Hawk later described the scene of the massacre:

General Edmund Gaines commanded the 1,600 Illinois volunteers who sought to drive Black Hawk from the state. Undisciplined and untrained, the volunteers only worsened the crisis, which might otherwise have been settled peacefully. One of the officers in the volunteers was a young lawyer from New Salem named Abraham Lincoln, who reported engaging in a "good many bloody struggles with the mosquitos" but none with any "live, fighting Indians."

Attempting to flee Illinois across the Mississippi River, Black Hawk and his followers, including many women and children, were caught at that great waterway's confluence with the Bad Axe River. Their attempts to surrender were ignored, and the ensuing massacre left the Mississippi "perceptibly tinged with the blood of the Indians who were shot in its margin and in the stream," according to one white eyewitness.

Early in the morning a party of whites came upon our people, who were attempting to cross the Mississippi. They tried to give themselves up— the whites paid no attention to their entreaties—but commenced slaughtering them. In a little while the whole army arrived. Our braves, but few in number, finding that the enemy paid no regard to age or sex, and seeing that they were murdering helpless women and little children, determined to fight until they were killed. As many women as could, commenced swimming the Mississippi, with their children on their backs. A number of them were drowned, and some shot, before they could reach the opposite shore.

General Joseph Street, a participant in the assault, described the massacre at Bad Axe in similar terms. He wrote:

The Indians were pushed literally into the Mississippi, the current of which was at one time perceptibly tinged with the blood of the Indians who were shot on its margin and in the stream. It is impossible to say how many Indians have been killed, as most of them were shot in the water or drowned in attempting to cross the Mississippi.

After the massacre, the survivors resumed their journey to Iowa. But Black Hawk did not accompany them. Instead,

Black Hawk escaped from the slaughter at the Bad Axe and slipped away into Wisconsin, only to be forced to surrender (depicted here) when betrayed by some Winnebagos with whom he had sought shelter. After a year in prison, he spent some of his days before his death in 1838 as a kind of traveling tourist attraction in the cities of the East.

Whirling Thunder, the oldest son of Black Hawk, accompanied his father when he finally surrendered to U.S. government forces at Prairie du Chien.

he went to a nearby Winnebago village and requested that several Winnebago leaders escort him to the Americans so that he could surrender. Finally, on August 27, 1832, Black Hawk arrived at the American town of Prairie du Chien and surrendered to General Joseph Street. He was accompanied by his eldest son, Nasheaskuk (Whirling Thunder), an aide named Neapope (Broth), and the Winnebago leader Wabokieshiek.

Black Hawk and his companions were sent to a military post called Jefferson Barracks. As they were traveling to the Barracks, Black Hawk thought about the recent events:

> On our way down, I surveyed the country that had cost us so much trouble, anxiety, and blood, and that now caused me to be a prisoner of war. I reflected upon the ingratitude of the whites, when I saw their fine houses, rich harvests, and every thing desirable around them; and recollected that all this land had been ours, for which me and my people had never received a dollar, and that the whites were not satisfied until they took our village and our grave-yards from us, and removed us across the Mississippi.

Thus ended the conflict known as the Black Hawk War. It lasted only a few short months and resulted in the permanent removal of the Sac from their homeland east of the Mississippi River. By then, all of the Sac and Fox had resettled in Iowa. The war signaled the end of effective resistance to the onslaught of American settlers into the territory once held by the Sac and Fox in Illinois. ▲

The garb worn by Moses Keokuk and his son Charles for this 1868 photographic portrait illustrates the opposing cultural forces that were at work on the Sac and Fox in the later decades of the 19th century.

THE
DISPOSSESSED

During the period between 1832 and 1867, the Sac and Fox were compelled to make many changes in their lives. By 1832, they had relocated from their traditional homeland in Illinois to territory in Iowa. They later resettled twice more, first from Iowa to Kansas, and finally to Oklahoma. During this time, the Sac and Fox came under increasing pressure to accept certain aspects of American culture. They were able, however, to retain many of their valued traditions.

In the month following the end of the Black Hawk War, Governor John Reynolds of Illinois called Sac and Fox leaders to a meeting to discuss the consequences of Black Hawk's defeat. The meeting took place on September 19, 1832. Reynolds wanted to obtain land cessions from the Sac and Fox. He was well aware that he was in an advantageous position to force the chiefs to come to terms. As he noted to his aides, "The

power to dictate terms is very much in our hands."

When Reynolds spoke to the Sac and Fox chiefs, he demanded that they sell a portion of their territory lying on the western side of the Mississippi River. Although the chiefs resisted at first, they finally agreed to sell a strip of land 60 miles wide along the Mississippi in the state of Iowa. The territory consisted of some 6 million acres.

In exchange for the Indians' land, the U.S. government promised to pay the Sac and Fox an annuity of $2,000 for a period of 30 years. The total payment for the land was $60,000, even though the land was worth more than $7 million at that time.

American settlers continued to encroach on Indian lands in the Midwest. They built many towns in Iowa, near the territory of the Sac and Fox. Only one year after the end of the Black

Hawk War, Black Hawk himself commented on the people's predicament:

> I have since found the country much settled by the whites near to our people, on the west side of the river. I am very much afraid, that in a few years, they will begin to drive and abuse our people, as they have formerly done. I may not live to see it, but I feel certain that the day is not distant.

Indeed, that day was soon to arrive.

Shortly after the Sac and Fox agreed to sell some of their territory in Iowa, the U.S. government asked for even more land. In September 1836, Sac and Fox chiefs signed an agreement to sell 400 square miles of their land in payment of debts that the people owed to American merchants at trading posts. A Sac leader who participated in the agreement noted, "We are unable to end the great fog of white people which is rolling toward the setting sun."

Just one year later, Sac and Fox leaders signed another treaty in Washington, D.C. In the Treaty of 1837, the Sac and Fox ceded an additional 1.25 million acres next to the tract that they had sold the previous year. In return, they received $100,000 and a small annuity.

The Treaty of 1837 contained several additional provisions that affected the lives of the Sac and Fox. It stated that the American government would send teachers and ministers to Sac and Fox villages. Government officials wanted the teachers to instruct Indian children about American society and culture.

They wanted to teach the children to adopt American values. And they hoped that American education would convince Sac and Fox children to abandon their own traditions and beliefs.

In accordance with these goals, a number of schools were established in Sac and Fox communities. Ministers belonging to several Protestant sects also hoped to change the lives and beliefs of the Sac and Fox. They wanted to convert the people to Christianity.

The Sac and Fox allowed the teachers and missionaries to come to their villages. But few parents sent their children to the schools, and few people attended the ministers' religious services.

As the Sac and Fox experienced greater contact with American settlers, teachers, and missionaries, new problems arose in their communities. Even their health was seriously and tragically affected. The Sac and Fox contracted diseases of European origin such as smallpox, measles, and influenza. These diseases proved deadly to many of the Sac and Fox. The people had no natural immunities or resistances to the diseases because they had not previously been exposed to the organisms that cause them. These organisms did not exist in North America before European contact. Several devastating epidemics of smallpox and measles spread throughout the Sac and Fox villages in the middle of the 19th century. The population of Sac and Fox, which totaled approximately 6,000 in 1833, was reduced to 2,400 by 1846.

In the early 1840s, the U.S. government renewed its demand that the Sac

Once the Sac and Fox were forced onto government reservations, the opportunities for them to practice their traditional means of subsistence, such as hunting, were severely diminished.

and Fox sell all of their remaining land in Iowa. At a meeting between the government and Sac and Fox leaders, the Americans convinced the Indians to leave Iowa and move farther west, preferably to Kansas. One official who had visited the Sac and Fox in 1832 commented on their situation in 1841: "What a melancholy difference nine years have made among them."

Once again, Sac and Fox leaders initially resisted the government's demands. The Fox voiced even stronger opposition to further sales of land than did the Sac. The Fox did not want to leave their territory in Iowa because they knew that it was much better farmland than they would find in Kansas. The United States commissioner of Indian affairs, Carey Harris, knew it too. He commented that the land of the Sac and Fox in Iowa was "as fine land as the world can produce."

However, as in the past, the Sac and Fox finally agreed to move because they knew that they had no real choice. They realized that American officials would never prevent settlers from intruding on Sac and Fox territory.

In the Treaty of 1842, the Sac and Fox sold their remaining land in Iowa for the sum of $258,566.34. They also received an annual payment of 5 percent interest on a sum of $800,000 that the United States government held in a trust account. The Sac and Fox agreed to move to land west of the Missouri River in the present-day state of Kansas. According to the treaty's terms, the Sac and Fox were given until May 1, 1843, to leave the eastern half of their territory in Iowa. They pledged to move from the remainder by 1845.

After the first move was made from the eastern portion of their land, a group of Fox rejected the terms of the Treaty of 1842. Their leader, a man named Poweshiek, objected to the agreement. He and his people decided to return to their former territory in Iowa. Between 1843 and 1844, they twice went back to their villages on the Iowa River. But both times, American authorities sent a force of militia to evict them.

In compliance with the Treaty of 1842, the Sac and Fox resettled on 435,200 acres of land along the Osage River in Kansas. There they lived with other Indians from the Ottawa, Chippewa, and Kansas nations. These peoples had previously relocated to Kansas from their own traditional lands.

As the Sac and Fox adjusted to their new territory, they tried to maintain their traditional way of life. But their situation presented them with numerous problems. First of all, the land of the Sac and Fox in Kansas consisted mostly of dry prairie. Sac and Fox women had a difficult time turning the earth into productive farmland. Although the women continued to plant their crops,

the harvests were not adequate to support the people. In addition, there were few animals in the region for the men to hunt. Therefore, Sac and Fox men spent less time hunting and fishing than when they had lived in Illinois and Iowa.

Since the Sac and Fox could not obtain enough food from their land or nearby resources, they relied on the provisions and annuities that the United States government had promised to give them in the treaties signed between the two nations. But the Sac and Fox could not prosper in the poor conditions in which they found themselves.

A second problem arose for the Sac and Fox as they became involved in conflicts with other Indian peoples in the region. The conflicts resulted from competition among Indians over the few resources available to them. Sac and Fox men had to travel north and west of their villages in order to hunt buffalo, deer, and other animals. As they did so, they entered the hunting territories of such Indians as the Lakota, Kiowa, Comanche, and Arapaho. These peoples objected to the presence of the Sac and Fox in their region. Raids occasionally occurred, with increasing hostilities and casualties on all sides.

However, the Sac and Fox had an important advantage in these conflicts. They had obtained guns and ammunition from European and American traders. At that time, most of the Indians in the Plains did not have access to guns but relied instead on bows and arrows. The Sac and Fox were therefore better equipped for warfare.

In this 1837 portrait, the Fox chief Poweshiek looks proud and formidable, but just two years earlier his people, as well as the Sac and their neighbors the Ojibwa, Menomini, Iowa, Santee Sioux, Winnebago, Ottawa, and the Potawatomi, had been forced to agree that the U.S. government could make ''an amicable and final adjustment'' of their various land claims. In the 1840s, Poweshiek was among the Sac and Fox leaders who advocated a return to their lands in Iowa.

A rare photograph of Sac and Fox leaders, including Keokuk (seated, second from left), as they conclude treaty negotiations with U.S. government officials in 1867. By terms of the treaty, the Sac and Fox were compelled to sell the government 157,000 acres of fertile farmland in Iowa between the Mississippi and Missouri rivers in exchange for little more than $26,000 and a 750-acre reservation in the Indian Territory of Oklahoma.

Throughout the middle of the 19th century, epidemics of cholera, smallpox, and measles continued to plague the Sac and Fox. Many people died from these diseases. In a short period of only 20 years, nearly half of their population of approximately 2,400 died from the epidemics.

As their situation worsened, the unity of the Sac and Fox communities was threatened. Some people wanted to follow their traditional ways of living as much as possible. They were led by the Fox chief Mokohoko. Another group favored acceptance of American values and behaviors. The Sac leader Keokuk headed this faction. Keokuk supported the introduction of American schools and missions in Sac and Fox villages. He encouraged people to send their children to schools. He formed a friendship with a group of Quakers, who then established a school and church in the Sac community in 1859. However, few of the Sac and Fox attended the school or church.

Disagreements arose between the Sac and the Fox as well. Since the Fox had remained neutral during the Black Hawk War, they felt that they were unjustly punished by the American government for events in which they had not participated. They blamed the Sac for the subsequent loss of land and forced relocations.

In 1851 and 1852, a group of approximately 100 Fox left their communities in Kansas and returned to Iowa. They were led by a chief named Mowmenwahnecah. Although both the Sac and the U.S. government tried to persuade these people to go back to Kansas, the renegade band of Fox refused. They were well received by some of the Americans then living in Iowa, although the Americans' motives were mostly selfish. Traders and merchants welcomed the opportunity to sell goods to the Fox, who had funds from an annuity amounting to $51,000. And American farmers were glad to hire the Fox at low wages to work as farm laborers at harvest time.

In 1856, the Fox in Iowa asked the state legislature to officially recognize their right to remain in the state. The legislature approved the Fox's request. The Fox then purchased 80 acres of land near Tama, Iowa, for a sum of $1,000. There they established a settlement called Mesquakie.

In the 1850s, American officials began to pressure the Sac and Fox to sell their territory in Kansas. The government ignored the treaties it had signed to protect the new lands of the Sac and Fox. Bowing to the pressure, the Sac and Fox sold a small portion of their land to the government. But their concession did not stop officials from demanding more land, and increasing numbers of American settlers encroached on the Sac and Fox territory in Kansas.

During this period, the U.S. Congress enacted legislation known as the Kansas-Nebraska Bill. It provided for the removal of Indians from Kansas and Nebraska. The bill stated that these peoples would be resettled in a region

One of the most tragic consequences of the relocation of Native American tribes to reservations was the end of their self-sufficiency. Hunters and agriculturalists alike now became dependent on government rations and supplies.

The stubborn Mokohoko advocated a return to the Sac and Fox lands in Iowa, but he attracted only a small band of followers. This photograph of his encampment was taken in the 1880s.

known then as Indian Territory, now the state of Oklahoma. Although the Kansas-Nebraska Bill became law in 1855, some members of Congress opposed it. Senator Edward Everett of Massachusetts spoke out against the mistreatment of Indians by the United States government. He said, "If we must use the tyrant's plea of necessity and invade the 'permanent home' of these children of sorrow and oppression, I hope that we shall treat them with more than justice, with more than equity, with the utmost kindness and tenderness."

In the House of Representatives, a congressman from Vermont voiced his protest. He stated that the Indians had already suffered from being taken away "from all that was delightful in the present, and sacred and glorious in the recollections of the past."

In 1859, the United States commissioner of Indian affairs, John Greenwood, met with Sac and Fox leaders. The group was headed by Moses Keokuk, a son of the Fox chief Keokuk. The Sac and Fox signed a new treaty in which they agreed to sell 300,000 acres of their land to American settlers. The treaty also stated that the remaining Sac and Fox territory would be divided into separate parcels, or allotments, consisting of 80 acres each. Every Sac and Fox resident was to receive an allotment.

The Sac and Fox objected to the division of their land because they believed that land should be owned in common by the group as a whole. However, American authorities pressured the people to accept allotments. An agent from the U.S. Bureau of Indian Affairs claimed that "large annuities in money and property held in common are drawbacks upon the Indians' advancement to civilization."

In response to mounting pressure from the American government, Sac and Fox leaders signed another treaty with the United States in 1867. They agreed to give up all of their territory in Kansas in exchange for acreage in the Indian Territory. The Sac and Fox pledged to leave Kansas and resettle in their new land by 1869.

But American settlers did not wait for the Sac and Fox to leave. They immediately began to move into Sac and Fox territory in Kansas. As in the past, American officials ignored the Indians when they protested the settlers' incursions on their land.

Shortly after the newest treaty was signed, some of the Fox rejected the agreement. A group of approximately 300 went back to their former lands in Iowa. They were led by the Fox chief Mokohoko, who had refused to sign the Treaty of 1867. He had always been an outspoken leader who resisted the demands of American officials for Sac and Fox land. Mokohoko and his group joined the Fox community of Mesquakie, which had been established in the early 1850s.

In 1869, the Sac and Fox made their final relocation. They departed on a journey that took them 19 days, traveling in wagons, on horseback, and on foot. They arrived in Oklahoma in December 1869 during a heavy snowstorm. The Sac and Fox settled on land that they purchased from the Choctaw, an Indian group that had previously been forced to move from their own territory in the Southeast.

The Sac and Fox obtained a total of 480,000 acres of land in Oklahoma. However, less than 10 percent of the land was good for farming. Despite the poor conditions of the soil, Sac and Fox women tried to maintain their traditional economies. They planted and harvested crops, but the land yielded very little. The men still went out to hunt buffalo, but the number of animals was greatly reduced. The hunters were rarely able to kill enough buffalo to fulfill the people's needs.

Although each Sac and Fox received an annuity share of $60, this money was insufficient for their support. In order to gain an income to purchase food and goods, some of the Sac and Fox began to lease land to American farmers and ranchers.

In the 1870s, a small group of Sac and Fox returned to Kansas. The Fox chief Mokohoko left Iowa and joined the people in Kansas. The United States government objected to the Fox's return to Kansas. In 1875, Mokohoko went to Washington, D.C., to meet with President Ulysses S. Grant to discuss the controversy. Grant told Mokohoko that he and his group must leave Kansas. The army sent a militia to the community and forcibly removed them to Oklahoma. However, the people immediately returned to Kansas.

The Sac and Fox in Oklahoma attempted to convince the Fox in Kansas to join them in Oklahoma. In 1886, a delegation of Sac and Fox went to Kansas to speak with the people there. Some of the Fox agreed to return to Oklahoma but others remained in Kansas. The people who remained were led by a chief named Pawshepawho, who had been their leader since the death of Mokohoko in 1878.

Shortly after the Sac and Fox resettled in Oklahoma, the U.S. government instituted a national policy of dividing Indian land into individual allotments. This policy differed, of course, from the traditional Sac and Fox method of land ownership, wherein, according to custom, land belonged to the people as a whole and not to individuals. Every member of the community could make use of the land as they needed.

The U.S. government had a negative view of the Indians' traditions. Officials believed that land should be owned by separate families or individuals. In accordance with this practice, the government wanted the Sac and Fox to divide their land into small allotments and assign each one to a separate family.

In order to achieve this goal, in 1887, the United States Congress passed the General Allotment Act, also known as the Dawes Act after its principal sponsor. The Dawes Act stated that land on Indian reservations should be divided into allotments consisting of 160 acres for a family and 80 acres for an individual living alone. The Dawes Act further specified that after all the land on a reservation had been allotted among residents, any surplus acreage could be sold to American settlers.

The Dawes Act also stated that allotments were to be held in trust for a period of 25 years. During that time, an individual owner could not sell his or her land. But when the trust period ended, the owner could sell the land if he or she chose to do so.

Most of the Sac and Fox objected to the policy of allotting land to individuals. A delegation, led by Charles Keokuk, grandson of Keokuk, went to Washington, D.C., to lodge their protests with American officials. The officials refused to change their policy.

The provisions of the Dawes Act were enforced on the Sac and Fox reservation in August 1891. The reservation was divided into 549 allotments assigned to residents. The surplus land was then sold to Americans. Money received from these sales was divided among every member of the Sac and Fox nation. Each share amounted to $250.

After allotments were assigned in 1891, the Sac and Fox in Oklahoma made

A late 19th-century photograph of Sac and Fox second-graders at the reservation school. By the terms of the Treaty of 1867, the U.S. government committed itself to providing a school on the Sac and Fox reservation.

Sac and Fox students at the U.S. Indian Agency school on the reservation in 1891.
Many Indians regarded the school as an agent for forcible assimilation into white society
that operated to hasten the destruction of Sac and Fox culture.

a payment of $100,000 to the Fox community in Iowa in order to cancel any claims to land or income by the people in Iowa. In later years, residents of the Iowa community asked for a larger payment. They appealed to federal officials to grant them an additional $450,000. The U.S. Supreme Court finally issued a ruling against the Iowa Fox in 1911, rejecting any further claims.

By the end of the 19th century, the lives of the Sac and Fox had changed considerably. Still, they tried to maintain their traditional ways of living as much as possible. Most of the people resisted the government's attempts to pressure the Sac and Fox to alter their values and beliefs. Several boarding schools were established on the reservation in Oklahoma, but few parents sent their children to them. And many of the children who were brought to school managed to run away and return home. The main school on the reservation concentrated on teaching manual labor skills. Boys were taught to build fences, tend cattle, and grow corn. Girls were instructed in cooking, sewing, and washing. These were the tasks that American authorities believed were proper for men and women. The Sac and Fox, however, objected to the emphasis placed on manual labor. And they did not approve of the regimented living conditions in the dormitories at school.

The Sac and Fox also objected to the fact that most of the teachers were religious missionaries. The missionaries were intolerant of Sac and Fox customs and beliefs. Instead, they tried to convert the children and adults to Christianity. However, their mission work met with very little success.

The Sac and Fox faced numerous problems in their efforts to improve their lives. They wanted to be productive farmers, but since the soil was of very poor quality, their harvests were insufficient to fulfill the people's needs. Even President Grover Cleveland recognized this problem. In a speech delivered in 1894, he warned that "in these days when the white agriculturalists and stock raisers of experience and intelligence find their lot a hard one, we ought not to expect Indians to support themselves on the small tracts of land usually allotted to them."

In addition to problems resulting from the condition of the soil on their land, the Sac and Fox had little money to buy modern farm equipment or make capital investments in their land. Few people could obtain loans from nearby banks because of the Americans' prejudice toward Indians.

The Sac and Fox continued to suffer from epidemic diseases. In 1899, a severe smallpox epidemic swept through the community. Health officials ordered the quarantine of several villages. Many houses and possessions were burned in order to stop the spread of disease.

So as the 19th century drew to a close, the Sac and Fox had made some difficult adjustments to their new land. They overcame numerous hardships in establishing some measure of stability and security in their lives. And, despite the pressures to abandon their customs, most of the people followed their valued traditions. ▲

Native American children at a powwow in Mesquakie, Iowa. Poverty and limited educational and economic opportunities are among the problems that confront today's generation of Sac and Fox.

THE
SAC
AND
FOX
TODAY

Changes in the circumstances of the Sac and Fox in the 20th century have led to their adoption of many aspects of American culture. However, the Sac and Fox have remained a distinct community and have maintained some of their unique traditions.

During the early years of the century, the Sac and Fox in Oklahoma continued to face problems in establishing prosperity. The land yielded small harvests, and the people had few alternative resources to depend upon. In 1903, Ross Griffin, the United States agent who administered the reservation, commented that "not a single Indian family is self-supporting on a farm."

The Sac and Fox maintained their traditional system of leadership into the 20th century. Chiefs met in councils to discuss matters of importance to their community. The people respected their advice and judgment.

However, the U.S. government attempted to change the political system on the reservation. Officials wanted the Sac and Fox to eliminate the chiefs' councils and replace them with a business committee. Most of the Sac and Fox opposed this new system. In 1909, American authorities sponsored a referendum on the reservation to decide on the future form of government. But very few people went to the polls to vote. Of 135 eligible voters, only 80 people participated. Forty-nine of these voted to keep the traditional council of chiefs, 10 voted to abolish the council, and the remaining 21 abstained. Despite the fact that the majority of voters wished to keep their traditional system, the secretary of the interior unilaterally abolished the council of chiefs. In its place, he appointed three men as members of the new business committee.

Most of the Sac and Fox tried to maintain other aspects of their traditional culture. Well into the 20th century, approximately half of the people followed their indigenous religious beliefs

This photograph of the sawmill on the Sac and Fox reservation was taken in 1890. Today, lack of economic development and a corresponding shortage of employment opportunities continue to plague the reservation.

and practices. And most of the people spoke their native language.

Still, other aspects of life were influenced by American society. A greater number of Sac and Fox children attended schools than in the previous century. Children were sent to boarding schools on the reservation. In addition, some children attended schools established for Indians in other parts of the country. They traveled 300 miles to the Haskell Institute in Lawrence, Kansas. Even farther away was the Carlisle Indian School located in Carlisle, Pennsylvania. Both Haskell and Carlisle offered academic and vocational training to Indians. The two schools were superior to the small local schools on the Sac and Fox Reservation.

As a result of difficulties in producing food or obtaining funds, many of the Sac and Fox sold their individual shares of land to American ranchers and farmers when the trust period for allotments ended. By 1919, 345 of the original 549 allotments were sold.

Without land, Sac and Fox men and women tried to obtain employment in order to have the money to buy food, clothing, and other essential goods. But there were few jobs available nearby. Most of the jobs were in farm work. Many Sac and Fox went to work as laborers on farms and ranches that occupied the territory they themselves had once owned.

In 1912, American gas and oil companies began to operate their industry in Oklahoma. They asked the Sac and Fox to allow them to explore for oil and gas on land owned by the tribe. The Sac and Fox agreed to lease some of their land to the companies. Income from these leases amounted to approximately $25,000 per year.

Despite this income and the jobs obtained by some residents of the Sac and Fox reservation, most of the people remained quite poor. Living conditions were difficult. Many people had to cope with a lack of adequate running water, heat, or electricity.

In the middle 1920s, the United States Senate sponsored a nationwide review of living conditions on Indian reservations. A commission of inquiry visited reservations and documented the situation of the people there. In 1928, the commission issued a lengthy report, known as the Merriam Report. It

For several decades spanning the late 19th century and early 20th century, many Sac and Fox children were sent to be educated at the famous Carlisle Indian School in Carlisle, Pennsylvania. This photograph shows the 1888 student body.

Perhaps the most famous graduate of the Carlisle Indian School was the great Sac and Fox athlete Jim Thorpe, who is considered by many to be the greatest all-around athlete in American history.

detailed the widespread poverty on reservations throughout the nation. It supplied evidence of a poor standard of living, high rates of unemployment and underemployment, lack of health services, and inadequate educational opportunities. The Sac and Fox were among the native groups suffering the most from these conditions.

In response to the findings of the Merriam Report, the commissioner of Indian affairs, John Collier, developed a policy to help improve the lives of American Indians. He wanted the people to have more control over their reservations and their resources. He wanted the federal government to provide additional funds to develop economic projects on reservations and to improve the people's living conditions.

Collier persuaded the United States Congress to enact legislation to implement his policies. In 1934, Congress passed the Indian Reorganization Act (IRA), which provided for the establishment of elected tribal councils and formal constitutions on all of the reservations. Congress also supplied funds to help reservation communities improve the lives of their people.

Two years after passage of the IRA, the legislature of the state of Oklahoma enacted the Oklahoma Indian Welfare Act. This act implemented the provisions of the IRA throughout the state. It called for constitutions and tribal councils on reservations in Oklahoma. The Sac and Fox adopted their own constitution in 1936. The constitution set out rules for the functioning of a local government on the reservation. The Sac and Fox also instituted a tribal council consisting of an elected chief and councillors. The Sac and Fox are presently governed by a council of five members who are elected to two-year terms.

In 1937, the residents of the Sac and Fox reservation at Mesquakie in Tama, Iowa, also adopted a constitution under the provisions of the Indian Reorganization Act. They are currently governed by two sets of representatives. They have a council composed of hereditary clan chiefs, in keeping with their traditional system of leadership. In addition, the people elect members to a business committee, which oversees community projects.

Many changes have come to the lives of Sac and Fox men and women in the 20th century. As in the past, though, problems remain in making use of the land. In Oklahoma, poor soil and little rainfall continue to impede the development of farming. Most of the Sac and Fox have adopted many features of American culture.

The people at Mesquakie in Iowa have maintained important aspects of their indigenous culture. Many of the religious practices are followed, including the clan ceremonies associated with sacred bundles. And a large number of the residents speak the Fox language.

Some of the Sac and Fox have left their reservations in Oklahoma, Iowa, and Kansas to seek jobs in towns and cities in their state and elsewhere in the United States. Those who remain on the reservations work in a wide variety of rural and urban occupations. Rates of unemployment are fairly high, however. For the Sac and Fox in Iowa, the unemployment rate for 1991 was 28 percent. Among the Sac and Fox in Kansas and Nebraska, the rate was somewhat lower, at approximately 20 percent. In Oklahoma, the unemployment rate reached as high as 59 percent.

Several members of the Sac and Fox community have gained international reputations in their professional fields. One was William Jones, who received a Ph.D. in anthropology from Columbia University in New York City. Dr. Jones went on to a successful career in research and writing. He published numerous articles and books dealing with the languages and culture of the Sac and Fox.

Perhaps the best-known resident of the Sac and Fox reservation was Jim Thorpe, the world-famous athlete and spokesperson for his people. Thorpe won two Olympic gold medals for the pentathlon and decathlon at the 1912 Olympic Games held in Stockholm, Sweden. The pentathlon consists of five track and field events. The decathlon is the most difficult of all, combining ten track-and-field competitions.

Thorpe impressed the world with his athletic ability and his informal and engaging personality. When King Gustav V of Sweden awarded the gold medals to Thorpe at the Olympic ceremony, the king said: "Sir, you are the greatest athlete in the world." Thorpe replied: "Thanks, King."

Controversy soon followed Thorpe's triumph at the Olympics. In 1913, the

John Bear looks under the hood of his vintage automobile. Today's Sac and Fox must find a way to adapt their traditional values to the demands of modern society.

American Athletic Union (AAU) claimed that Thorpe had played professional baseball in 1910, two years prior to the Olympic competition. It said that since he had been a paid athlete before the Olympics, he did not qualify as an amateur and therefore should not have competed in the Games. Thorpe denied that he had violated the Olympic rules because he had only played ball in the minor leagues for a brief time during a summer vacation and had not received a regular salary. The AAU did not change its ruling and forced Thorpe to return the two gold medals he had won in Stockholm.

Later in his professional baseball and football career, Jim Thorpe received several important honors from the sports world. In 1950, an Associated Press poll of sports writers named Thorpe as the "Greatest Football Player of the Half-Century." Another AP poll of the same year called him the "Greatest Athlete of the Half-Century." In 1951, a motion picture was made of his life. Entitled *Jim Thorpe, All-American*, it depicted his career and triumphs as an athlete.

At that time, a committee was formed to try to restore Jim Thorpe's Olympic medals. Thorpe died a few years later, in 1953, but the committee continued its efforts on his behalf. Twenty years later, in 1973, the AAU restored Thorpe's amateur status for the period from 1909 to 1912. Finally, in 1982, the International Olympic Committee returned Jim Thorpe's two gold medals to his family.

Today there are three Sac and Fox reservations in the United States. The populations of the reservations have grown steadily in this century. The largest is on the reservation in Oklahoma. In 1990, the United States Bureau of the Census reported that 4,704 Sac and Fox reside on the reservation. This figure includes 2,407 women and 2,297 men. The reservation itself consists of 15,072 acres of land allotted to individuals. An additional 970 acres are tribally owned.

The next in size is the Mesquakie Settlement in Tama, Iowa. Its population is

Even today, pride in their traditions and values remains the foundation of the Sac and Fox identity.

564, including 277 women and 287 men. Mesquakie now contains 3,300 acres of land, which is an increase of more than 2,000 acres from its original size in the middle of the 19th century. It has grown through several purchases of land made by the Sac and Fox residents. All of the land at Mesquakie is owned in common by the tribe.

Stepping out of the shadows: many times in the past, the destruction of the Sac and Fox has seemed imminent, yet the people continue to endure.

The smallest of the Sac and Fox reservations is the one located in the adjacent counties of Brown County, Kansas, and Richardson County, Nebraska. It has 49 Sac and Fox residents. Of these, 31 are women, while 18 are men. The reservation consists of 80 acres of allotted land.

The median age of the populations on all three Sac and Fox reservations is relatively young. In Kansas and Nebraska, the median age is approximately 15 years. At the Mesquakie Settlement in Iowa, the median age is 22 years. It is somewhat older in Oklahoma, at 25 years. A low median age is a good sign for the future. It indicates that the population of Sac and Fox will continue to increase.

As the Sac and Fox look to the future, they will undoubtedly make strides in improving the lives of their people. Many of the problems they face are due to their rural environment and to the effects of their complex history. Sac and Fox ancestors were dispossessed of beautiful, fertile lands as American set-tlers ignored the indigenous people's claims to their own territory. The Sac and Fox today are still coping with the consequences of past events. But their knowledge of the importance of unity and tradition will no doubt enable them, in the future, to survive, succeed, and even thrive as a people. ▲

BIBLIOGRAPHY

Bauxer, J. Joseph. "History of the Illinois Area." In *The Northeast*, edited by B. Trigger. Vol. 15, *Handbook of North American Indians*. Washington, D.C.: Smithsonian Institution Press, 1978.

Bernatos, Bob. *Jim Thorpe*. New York: Chelsea House, 1992.

Bonvillain, Nancy. *Black Hawk*. New York: Chelsea House, 1994.

Callender, Charles. "Fox." In *The Northeast*, edited by B. Trigger. Vol. 15, *Handbook of North American Indians*. Washington, D.C.: Smithsonian Institution Press, 1978.

————. "Great Lakes-Riverine Sociopolitical Organization." In *The Northeast*, edited by B. Trigger. Vol. 15, *Handbook of North American Indians*. Washington, D.C.: Smithsonian Institution Press, 1978.

————. "Sauk." In *The Northeast*, edited by B. Trigger. Vol. 15, *Handbook of North American Indians*. Washington, D.C.: Smithsonian Institution Press, 1978.

Hagan, William. *The Sac and Fox Indians*. Norman: University of Oklahoma Press, 1958.

Hunter, William. "History of the Ohio Valley." In *The Northeast*, edited by B. Trigger. Vol. 15, *Handbook of North American Indians*. Washington, D.C.: Smithsonian Institution Press, 1978.

Jackson, Donald, ed. *Black Hawk: An Autobiography*. Urbana: University of Illinois Press, 1964.

Jones, William. *Fox Texts*. Washington, D.C.: American Ethnological Society, 1907.

Josephy, Alvin. "The Rivalry of Black Hawk and Keokuk." In *The Patriot Chiefs: Chronicles of American Indian Resistance*. New York: Viking Press, 1958.

Michelson, Truman, ed. *The Autobiography of a Fox Woman*. Washington, D.C.: Bureau of American Ethnology, 1920. Fortieth annual report, 1918–1919.

THE SAC AND FOX AT A GLANCE

TRIBE   *Sac and Fox*
CULTURE AREA   *Northeast*
GEOGRAPHY   *Upper Midwest*
LINGUISTIC FAMILY   *Algonquian*
CURRENT POPULATION   *Approximately 5,300*
FEDERAL STATUS   *Recognized. Reservations in Oklahoma, Kansas and Nebraska, and Iowa*

GLOSSARY

agent A person appointed by the Bureau of Indian Affairs to supervise U.S. government programs on a reservation and/or in a specific region.

annuity Money or goods paid yearly or at a regular interval.

anthropology The scientific study of human beings and their culture.

breechcloth A strip of animal skin or cloth that is drawn between the legs and hung from a belt tied around the waist.

Bureau of Indian Affairs (BIA) A federal government agency, now within the Department of the Interior, founded to manage relations with Native American tribes.

clan A multigenerational group having a shared identity, organization, and property based on belief in their descent from a common ancestor. Because clan members consider themselves closely related, marriage within a clan is strictly prohibited.

confederacy A union of related tribes or nations that functions as a political, military, and/or economic unit.

conquistadores Spanish explorers who sought to conquer the New World.

council A meeting of group representatives for discussion or advice.

culture The learned behavior of humans; nonbiological, socially taught activities; the way of life of a group of people.

Dawes Act The 1887 federal law, also known as the General Allotment Act, that called for dividing reservation land into small allotments assigned to individual families. This policy undermined the traditional native way of life.

Great (or Gentle) Manitou A spirit in the sky who watches over the earth and its creatures; the Sac and Fox believed in many different spirits.

Indian Removal Act Legislation signed by President Andrew Jackson in 1830 that required many Indian tribes to relinquish their land in the East and move west of the Mississippi; it was applied to the Sac's situation.

Indian Reorganization Act (IRA) The 1934 federal law that allocated money for improvements on the reservations and promoted autonomous tribal governments.

indigenous Native to a particular region.

lacrosse A game in which players use a long-handled stick with netting on one end to catch and throw a ball to a goal.

lodge A long building constructed from a frame of arched wooden poles covered with bark; one rectangular lodge housed several related families.

missionary A member of a particular religious group who travels to different regions trying to convert others to his or her faith.

patrilineal descent A kinship system that traces descent from the father's side of the family.

peace chief A man chosen to be a civil leader because of his intelligence and good temper. Peace chiefs met in councils and offered advice to the community.

reservation A tract of land retained by Indians for their own occupation and use.

siege A military blockade of a city to force its surrender.

supplicant One who asks for something humbly and earnestly, as when praying to a higher power.

taboo A prohibition of certain actions because of social custom or fear of a supernatural power.

treaty A contract negotiated between nations that dealt with the cessation of military action, the surrender of political independence, the establishment of boundaries, terms of land sales, and related matters.

tribe A society consisting of several separate communities united by kinship, culture, language, and other social institutions, including clans, religious organizations, and warrior societies.

war chief A respected warrior from a specific clan who was chosen to plan and lead war expeditions and to supervise the village police.

PICTURE CREDITS

NANCY BONVILLAIN has a Ph.D. in anthropology from Columbia University. Dr. Bonvillain has written a grammar book and dictionary of the Mohawk language as well as *The Huron* (1989), *The Mohawk* (1992), *The Hopi,* and *Black Hawk* (1994) for Chelsea House. She has recently finished work on *Women and Men: Cultural Constructs of Gender.*

FRANK W. PORTER III, general editor of INDIANS OF NORTH AMERICA, is director of the Chelsea House Foundation for American Indian Studies. He holds a B.A., M.A., and Ph.D. from the University of Maryland. He has done extensive research concerning the Indians of Maryland and Delaware and is the author of numerous articles on their history, archaeology, geography, and ethnography. He was formerly director of the Maryland Commission on Indian Affairs and American Indian Research and Resource Institute, Gettysburg, Pennsylvania, and he has received grants from the Delaware Humanities Forum, the Maryland Committee for the Humanities, the Ford Foundation, and the National Endowment for the Humanities, among others. Dr. Porter is the author of *The Bureau of Indian Affairs* in the Chelsea House KNOW YOUR GOVERNMENT series.